Sarah B Adams

Amy and Marion's Voyage Around the World

Sarah B Adams

Amy and Marion's Voyage Around the World

ISBN/EAN: 9783337427702

Printed in Europe, USA, Canada, Australia, Japan

Cover: Foto ©Andreas Hilbeck / pixelio.de

More available books at **www.hansebooks.com**

Amy and Marion's Voyage Around the World.

BY
SARAH B. ADAMS.

BOSTON:
D. LOTHROP AND COMPANY,
FRANKLIN ST., CORNER OF HAWLEY.

CONTENTS.

	PAGE.
CHAPTER I.	
THEY EMBARK	7
CHAPTER II.	
OFF CAPE HORN	31
CHAPTER III.	
SAN FRANCISCO	56
CHAPTER IV.	
CROSSING THE PACIFIC . . .	76

CONTENTS.

CHAPTER V.
HONG KONG 105

CHAPTER VI.
TRIP TO CANTON 138

CHAPTER VII.
CANTON 171

CHAPTER VIII.
RETURN TO HONG KONG . . . 196

CHAPTER IX.
SAIGON AND SINGAPORE . . . 219

CHAPTER X.
SHANGHAI AND AMOY . . . 257

CHAPTER XI.
MACAO—HONG KONG 286

CHAPTER XII.
MANILA 319

CHAPTER XIII.

EXCURSION TO PAGSANJAN . . . 353

CHAPTER XIV.

HOMEWARD BOUND 373

AMY AND MARION'S VOYAGE AROUND THE WORLD.

CHAPTER I.

THEY EMBARK.

THE long summer vacation was over, and Mr. Clinton's school for young ladies was re-opened in No. 63 —— street, Boston, on the last Monday of September, 18—. That day was given up to the arrangement of seats and classes for the year, and no brain-work was done except by the gentleman who was preparing to resume his task, his life-work, which might be compared to the cultivation of thirty-two pieces of ground; some fertile and ready for the seed that should be sown, some naturally good, but choked with gaudy, useless weeds, and all different.

The weight of his responsibilities pressed so heavily upon Mr. Clinton as he reorganized his old classes, and found out how much knowledge the new pupils possessed, that when half-past eleven came he was glad to ring his bell and announce a half-hour recess.

The hubbub that ensued was worse than if ten beehives had been upset all at once.

"Where have you been all summer?" "Oh! at the Shoals. I had *such* fun!" "Newport is ever so much nicer, don't you think so?" "Isn't it dismal to come back here and grind all winter?" Questions and answers grew more and more emphatic, until one question seemed to prevail among a group of girls who were perched upon their desks, consuming cookies and doughnuts. "Where is Marion Gilmer? Isn't she coming back this year?"

"Marion Gilmer is down stairs, and says she has only come to get her books and say good-bye," said one who had come from the lower entry. A cry of disapprobation arose, and the said Marion entered in time to be complimented by it.

"Not coming here to school any more, Marion! Why not? You're not going to Miss Leighton's instead, you naughty girl?"

"Friends, do be quiet," said the favorite Marion. "Let me announce my solemn news. No more Virgil for me! Farewell to compositions upon the relation of the universe to the soul of man! I am going around the world in a great ship. I start next week for Cape Horn and the Antarctic Zone."

Her bewildered hearers could only entreat for further particulars.

"Why, the whole story is this: My cousin, Amy Roslyn, has a sailor brother, captain of the 'Lyra,' who is going to take her on his next voyage, and he asked Papa to let me go also, to keep her from being homesick. Papa meditated upon the subject, and wisely concluded that I might gain from the heathen world some education that would not be found in this House of Instruction and Correction, so he consented. Gussie Knowles knows all about it, for she is Amy's friend as well as mine, but I told her not to breathe a word of it to any of you, because I wanted the fun of coming in and making you stare." And Marion drew a long breath, while her face beaming with satisfaction implied that the fun had exceeded all her hopes.

Everybody congratulated and envied her, and commented variously upon Marion's great expectations.

"A voyage round Cape Horn to San Francisco, then to China and the East Indies! How romantic!" said Clara Hayes. "Won't you write to us, Marion?"

"Oh, dear girls! it would keep me writing the whole time to correspond with all of you; but Gussie Knowles will get long journal letters from us both, and she will read them to you;

but, oh! there's the bell, and I have not taken leave of Mr. Clinton. Good-bye, dear creatures." And Marion, escaping from overwhelming hugs, shook hands with her kind teacher, and left the halls of learning behind her with no regrets, but bright anticipations of the future.

Marion Gilmer and her cousin Amy Roslyn, were well adapted for a long voyage in each other's company, for there was a "harmonious difference" of character between them that is apt to form the basis of a true friendship; each admiring and depending upon the qualities in the other lacking in herself. Their letters and journals will give a better idea of each one, perhaps, than could any formal description; and a word sketch of Marion's round, merry face, short, solid figure, changeable gray eyes; of Amy's slender, graceful form, and sweet, pale face lighted up by brown eyes that could sparkle brilliantly with fun, or grow soft and hazy with musing, will give the outside view of these two girls who were about to enter together upon a chapter of their lives that was to be entirely different from any preceding one.

Their delight in the prospect of a voyage to strange, eastern lands nearly turned their heads during the weeks of preparation. With the assistance of sober-minded and practical friends, however, they managed to accomplish the necessary shopping and packing, and at last came a day when these helpful ones had performed their last offices for the young travellers, and were wandering mournfully about their deserted rooms, while in the clear October weather, with hopes as gay and bright as the autumn leaves, the girls went out to sea.

> Ship "LYRA," Atlantic Ocean,
> *October 30th.*

I begin to-day, dear old Gussie, my part of the joint journal-letter that Amy and I threatened to inflict upon you, for she says I shall describe the horrors of our first three days' experience in a far more graphic and touching manner than she ever could, and I do not consider it worth while to contradict her.

But first, I want you to realize how blissful we are at this present moment. Storms, Gulf Stream, and sea-sickness are things of the past; their memory only increases our comfort, for we are sailing through smooth blue waters; my ink-bottle stands safely on the wooden skylight that serves me as a writing table, and you may judge from that how calm the "wild Atlantic" is to-day.

Amy is stretched out in a great chair under the shadow of the "mizzen mast," for we are on "the house," (the roof of our large cabin which is sixty feet long, and the favorite resort of passengers), and every now and then she turns from her rapturous gazing at the quiet sea to take a bite of an apple, and exclaim: "Marion, this is truly bliss! This is worth that awful Gulf Stream!" Now I must really begin to tell you what our experience has been thus far.

The "Lyra" went out of New York harbor with a rousing breeze, and we were ready to scream with joy until we got near the Highlands of Navesink, for everything seemed perfect as possible,— our ship was such a fine one,— and the idea of our voyage grew more romantic with every mile,— or knot, for do let us be nautical in our terms.

Finally, Amy said: "Marion, I'm going down into the cabin to get another apple." "You will never come up if you do," was my solemn warning; but the rash girl departed, and when I reluctantly went in search of her, some time after, there she was, flat on her back in her berth. The first sight of her aroused within me feelings which, as Mark Twain says, were "peculiar, but not entertaining," but I put them down with stern determination, and went to the dinner-table, where the captain received me with commendations.

"You are a brave girl, Marion, and will make a fine sailor. Have some stewed onions?"

(advancing a spoonful of what looked like greasy seaweed). A silent shake of the head was the only answer on the part of the "brave girl and fine sailor." "Miss Gilmer looks pale," remarked Mr. Duncan, the mate, with a mischievous glance. "Nonsense! she isn't going to be sick. Why, Marion, my girl!" But the heroic young female was departing with more speed than dignity, and burst into her stateroom, crying to the prostrate sufferer in the lower berth: "Oh! Amy, I am sick! Oh! isn't it dreadful! What shall I do?" "Climb up into your berth, and lie down flat; the motion is growing worse and worse." So all that day there were two doleful beings in those narrow quarters, trying to comfort each other. The stewardess is Irish, and of all the funny women she might take the prize. Every little while she would enter, and balancing herself against the wall would observe: "Well, young ladies! I've come to see how ye was gettin' along," and then would come some anecdote of captains' wives and daughters whom she had attended through the most unheard of experiences, until, sick as we were, we had to laugh. The captain heard us, and shouted: "Well! I never heard seasick passengers make such cheerful sounds before. Girls, come out of that room. You are only —'making believe,' I know."

There was not much laughter in the "Lyra's" cabin on the following day, you may be assured, for we had a lively experience of the Gulf Stream under the influence of "a stiff nor'-easter" and enough queer things happened to amuse any girls not ill and half-scared as we were. I made a desperate venture, and in some ungraceful manner succeeded in reaching one of the cabin sofas (of which there are two in opposite alcoves), and clutching the mahogany ridge at the top to keep from sliding off, I lay all through that day, while the ship rolled in a way that any decent vessel would be ashamed of, except in the Gulf Stream.

Now and then a general crash enlivened me. I saw through the door that leads to the "forward cabin," our dining-room, various strange performances, such as a sugar barrel promenading the floor, and the stewardess falling down with a dish of pickles that bounced far and wide. Amy's state-room door opened, and a dishevelled maiden looked forth, longing to gain the opposite sofa, but fearing to attempt the passage across the cabin, which slanted like Somerset street hill, first in one direction, then in the other. She made a rush at last, and was thrown violently upon the sofa, from which soon after she was forcibly impelled, and fell with a startling thump upon the cabin floor as an unusually big wave struck the ship. At the moment of Amy's fall, everything that could follow her example did so; chairs upset, books tumbled out of the captain's shelf, and I was edified to behold Doddridge's "Rise and Progress" coasting across the cabin, pursued by an empty bottle and half-a-dozen apples from a plate on the sideboard.

I was not sick enough to want to be thrown into the sea, though I have a lurking suspicion that such was the case with poor Amy, but I felt very uncomfortably, and when a tall, shaggy-coated figure stood before me, and a cheery voice said: "Miss Gilmer, the captain says you must come on deck, for you are not sick enough to stay down here, and he won't allow it," I groaned in reply: "I can't think of such a thing."

Our first officer is a man of determination, and he at last succeeded in getting me on deck, where I sat on a wooden thing they call "the bumpkin," and held on for dear life to a "belaying pin," while I saw the great, green billows towering behind us and breaking in showers of spray; the vessel all the while prancing up and down like a rocking-horse. It was glorious, and I began to revive as the strong salt wind blew in my face, nearly taking my breath away.

Amy was longer than I in recovering, but now we are in a region of pleasant, moderate winds, where we can begin to enjoy sea-life in earnest. She tells me I have written enough for the present, and must let her take up the pen.

November 29th.

DEAR GUSSIE: I thought I would not continue this narrative till I had gained a more settled experience of sea-life, and now we are as much at home on this noble vessel as if we had sailed in her for months. I wish you could look in upon us and see how comfortable we are. Marion's account of our seasick days may lead you to think that we share one state-room, but it was only so at first, because "misery loves company." The captain has fitted up a separate room for her, and has taken away the upper berth from my room to give me plenty of light and air. The carpenter made me a set of shelves for books, and one small shelf for a kind of dressing-table is fastened to the wall under my looking-glass. I have pictures of all kinds adorning my walls, and some of the ferns that you and I gathered and pressed last summer, droop gracefully above them.

Our parlor, or "after-cabin," is quite a large, pleasant room, lighted by two windows and a skylight. Its walls are of a dark, polished mahogany; and a cabinet-organ, marble-topped centre-table, velvet sofas, easy chairs, and a Brussels carpet (very much faded), give it a homelike aspect. There are cupboards in the wall where we keep our work and boxes of sewing materials. Spare state-rooms are places of general stowage, and the captain has a little office leading from the parlor cabin, which is furnished with a great hair-cloth sofa, a desk, and many nautical instruments.

Thus you see, dear, that we can be very comfortable at sea, and I do not believe your imagination ever pictured such a view of cosiness on board of a ship as our cabin presents on a rainy evening when the swinging lamp sheds a soft light upon the captain in his reclining chair, listening to Amy playing on the organ, or to Marion reading aloud, while the pattering rain on the skylight and the dash of waves against the vessel's side, make us exclaim occasionally: "How comfortable we are! Where are the anticipated hardships of a sea-life?" My brother smiles significantly, as he replies: "They will come in time. We are not round the Horn, or near it yet."

We seldom have to spend an evening in the cabin, for moonlight or starlight nights are far more frequent than rainy ones, and we sit upon the house hearing the sailors' songs, when, at half-past seven the order "pump ship" is given, or we watch the stars, or the phosphorescence in our wake, or promenade the deck together. I must confess, though, that our chief occupation on pleasant evenings is to converse with the first and second mates, whichever happens to be "standing his watch" on deck, and you will doubtless hear enough of these worthies before our voyage is ended, to be glad of a description of their characteristics now, before I proceed with my narration.

Alexander Duncan, the first mate, is a very tall, broad-shouldered Scotchman, with a pleasant, sun-burnt face, whose frank blue eyes make you sure he is a person to be trusted. He is not very Scotch in his ways or accent,— rather Western, perhaps, for nearly all his life has been spent in Iowa when not at sea, and though he does not appear to have had the best educational and social advantages, he is so truly one of nature's noblemen, that a lack of external polish might be readily pardoned him.

Our second officer, Ned Fordyce, is a much more stylish individual than Mr. Duncan. He is the son of a wealthy Philadelphia merchant. Having completed his junior year at college he was obliged to give up study on account of severe headaches; therefore, as the sea had been his passion from boyhood, he chose a sailor's life, and rapidly worked his way up from the lowest position of a seaman to that which he now occupies. He is full of fun, and so entertaining that I wish we could have him at our table instead of the graver first mate; but it is the custom for the latter dignitary to eat with the captain, and there must always be one mate on deck to look after the ship.

Of our dear captain you need no description, for you know almost as well as I do, that no sister was ever blessed with a better brother than he has been to me, although during my childhood our intercourse was only occasional, because of his roving life. It is a great pleasure now to be with him all the time, gaining a more intimate friendship with the elder brother to whom my childish eyes used to look up as to the personification of everything noble and manly. I shall endeavor to let Marion do all the affectionate raving about him after this, for it will not sound so badly from a cousin as from his own sister.

Now the warm weather has come. We crossed the equator on the twenty-second of this month, and are in a region of pleasant breezes, which bear us gently on through the bluest water, specked here and there with foam. An awning over the deck where we sit makes a pleasant shade, and I am so lazy that to swing in a hammock and gaze at the fleecy clouds which float above the far horizon, is all that I am inclined to do a great part of the time, while my energetic cousin, whose faculties become stronger as the weather grows hotter, studies Latin with the captain, knits worsted garments for all her infant relatives (to be sent by mail from California when we arrive there), and reads to me when her eyes will allow it. The light on the water seems to affect them disagreeably, so she can not read or study long at a time; but I read to her generally, and she manages to entertain herself with something.

There is one hour of the day, Gussie, when I give my mental powers some work to do, whether they like it or not,— and that is from nine to ten A.M., at which time I take my seat at the table in our dining-room, and instruct Bob, the cabin-boy, in spelling, grammar, writing, and arithmetic. You know I always had a *penchant* for teaching, and if I should ever find it a necessity to earn my own living, that employment would be my choice. I find much enjoyment in this occupation, therefore, except on these warm, dreamy days, when it is a little hard for me to apply myself readily to anything.

I suppose you wondered how we kept Thanksgiving-day at sea. It was a very delightful day to me, for I never had more reason for thanksgiving. After long and frequent separations from my brother, to be sailing around the world with him and dear Marion seemed more like a dream of joy than a reality.

Our steward did himself credit by a dinner that was worthy of the day. Among the courses appeared salmon and green peas (canned), which, with the warm air, might have led us to think we were celebrating the fourth of July rather than the last Thursday in November. That evening was one of the most enchanting I ever knew. The golden and rosy clouds in the west were hardly faded when the full moon in the east threw a sheen over everything. Its light was not spectral, as we see it in our northern latitude, but something between golden and silvery, and it made the sails almost dazzling, while the intricate ropes were reflected on them with delicate tracery. We could see to read with the greatest ease. Being becalmed, there was scarcely a ripple on the sea, and we could discern a nautilus floating quietly along in the moonbeam's track, "trimming its lateen sail." All was breathless, seemingly, while the voices of the men came like the far-off sounds of a village when the day's work is ended. The night was what one might call intoxicating, and a wild ecstasy took possession of me, making me feel like doing almost anything extraordinary; so, to Marion's horror, I climbed out on the "channels" and sat there looking down into the water.

I do not know if I can make you understand what the channels are, but suffice it to say they look somewhat like shelves fastened to the outside of the ship, and to get out on them was a rash act more suited to Marion than to the quiet Amy. I took advantage of my brother being in the cabin in order to perform this great feat, but was interrupted in my pleasure by the alarmed Mr. Duncan who sprang forward, and begged "Miss Roslyn" to let him help her out of her dangerous position.

The sailors on the main deck were indulging in various sports, such as "hunt the slipper," or trotting out an imaginary horse,— one of the men on all fours, covered with sail-cloth, and ridden by another, who belabored his sides unmercifully. The stentorian voice of the boatswain would occasionally rise above the tumult in the refrain of some good Methodist hymn, for this man, a strong, fine-looking fellow, and one of the jolliest of the crew, is much addicted to hymn-singing, and sits in his room during many of his spare hours with his feet up on his blue chest, a pipe in one hand and a Wesleyan collection of hymns in the other, making melody that sadly interferes with the slumbers of those sailors who are taking their "watch below."

On Sundays every man in the ship (except the one at the wheel and the officer who is on duty), comes into the dining-room to attend the morning service, and an interesting sight it is, that row of men and boys, some rough, hard-looking characters, some with very intelligent faces,— with scarcely an exception, giving earnest, respectful attention to their young captain as he stands before them to read and explain the Word of God. Marion and I have to start the tunes, and I wish you could hear those men join in with all the strength of twenty-five pairs of lungs! I have always disliked the operatic singing by quartettes in many of our churches, as a mockery of the minister's words, when he rises to say "Let *us praise* God by singing the one hundred fifty-second hymn;" but when our sailors burst out with "I'm glad salvation's free," as if they know it is, and are glad of it, I think it comes nearer the right kind of worship.

We have passed many vessels since we left New York, and when they come near enough their captains carry on conversation with our captain by means of signal flags which are numbered. For example, a vessel sends up six, two, two, four, and by referring to our signal-book we see that those numbers indicate, "The Sovereign of the Seas;" then we tell them the name of this ship, and a great deal of information respecting the ports to which they are bound; from what port, how many days out, with what cargo, etc., is signalled between the ocean wayfarers, sometimes ending with the numbers six, three, eight, nine, from one vessel, that is, "Wish you a pleasant voyage;" and five, seven, eight, three, in reply, meaning "Many thanks."

Our great ensign was torn soon after we left New York, and I generously offered to devote my time and strength to its repairing, not realizing its size, for it doesn't look so monstrous when floating on the breeze far above us; but they all laughed when they saw me on a low stool with yards of red, white and blue bunting spreading from my lap far over the cabin floor, while I toiled with needle and thimble, feeling that I had undertaken quite a serious piece of business; and Marion, for a wonder in a lazy fit lay on the sofa watching my progress and declaring that she wouldn't take so many stitches to save every flag in the United States from ruin.

CHAPTER II.

OFF CAPE HORN.

MARION'S STORY.

December 8th.

WE are beginning to have cold weather now, although we still sit on deck nearly all the time, but in a few days the cabin will be our abiding place when we are engaged in our regular employments. Do you wish to hear what some of mine are? An account of yesterday's doings will give you a fair specimen of the way in which many of my days have been spent.

Directly after breakfast I burdened myself with the first volume of Prescott's "Ferdinand and Isabella," and swallowed my daily dose of history; then with my Latin books I went up to sit on the house and freeze my mortal frame in the sharp wind, while my mental powers combated with Virgil and the dictionary. I hope by the time I see my native shores to know more of Latin than I did in the *intelligere non possum* days,— which our schoolmate rendered "the possum is not an intelligent animal"— if the "pluck" which Mr. Fordyce compliments (after seeing me pore over my books with a visage like a thunder cloud,) will only hold out.

When that labor was over, finding that Arthur and Amy had left the cabin I went down to indulge in the rare opportunity of practising on the organ without any one to be agonized by the wails my uncultivated genius draws out of that small instrument. It isn't *too* sweet-toned at any time, and being used by mice as a boarding-house since it left Mason & Hamlin's Organ Rooms, has not improved its natural gifts. When I begin to blow I am not at all unlikely to see a long-tailed boarder rush out from under my feet; but I am not to be deterred by mice from learning to play my favorite tune, (the one in "Hymns Ancient and Modern," set to "Jerusalem the Golden"). Cousin Arthur comes in and watches my struggles with the keys and the bellows, pats me on the shoulder with the encouraging remark: "You'll learn some time, Breezie, don't despair;" but compassion for his and Amy's musical ears soon causes me to stop.

After dinner I allow myself the relaxation of reading Cooper's "Water Witch," or we gather in the captain's office, he reading aloud to us while we sew or draw. The evenings are growing very long as we come near the Cape, for December is midsummer with the Patagonians, and in two weeks I'm afraid it won't be dark enough for us to wish to go to bed all night long.

December 20th.

I am writing under very comical difficulties to-day, my dear, and does it not seem as if all the worst features of sea-life fall to my share in writing to you, leaving Amy only the descriptions of peaceful days and moonlight nights? The existing difficulties are that the low easy chair in which I have established myself takes an occasional promenade of about four feet from the table, which is fastened by iron staples to the floor, and has my inkstand tied upon it in a way that no one but our Captain Arthur would have thought of. There, now! a great roll of the ship! I hastily take a penful of ink and slide off in my chair, writing all the time; the next roll will bring me back to the table in time to dip my pen into the ink again.

A penetrating cold and dampness prevails, and the rolling and pitching will increase I suppose, till we are safely past Cape Horn. We have the funniest little stove imaginable in our parlor; eighteen inches in height, and eight in width, by actual measurement. There was an uproar of laughter from the passengers when the captain brought it out of obscurity to be our comfort in this cold region, and we soon found that we needn't expect much comfort from it, for it will not keep a fire alive more than ten minutes at a time, if not attended to as often as that, and the flame goes out like a flash on the slightest provocation. Now it is an impossibility for any mortal to remember every ten minutes to throw in two lumps of coal; consequently, we haven't attempted often to keep it up, and when the after-cabin becomes very chilly, we go into the dining-room and thaw by a generous stove that gives all the heat any frigid person could want. There we girls take no end of comfort, sitting cosily by the stove with our sewing, or writing by the table. One of the officers generally comes in when we are there (the one whose turn it happens to be to take his watch below), and spends an hour in playing chess with Amy, or I read aloud from a volume of Dickens while he sews. "While he sews!" I seem to hear you repeat in wonder. Yes! Mr. Duncan brings an old raisin box, wherein are collected divers implements of needle-work, and sits down with the utmost gravity to darn stockings, or put in patches, looking not a bit less manly than when he stands on deck to order the sailors, though I thought I should never stop laughing when I first saw him at that employment. The mother and sisters of Mr. Fordyce have fitted him out in style with a handsome sewing-case, but he doesn't handle his needle so skilfully as Mr. Duncan does, not having been obliged for so many years to take his own stitches. Do you think I am hard-hearted to let these poor fellows do their own darning and patching? Well, I do sew for them sometimes, and Mr. Duncan, not being used to have girls help him in these trifles, is so grateful when I propose it that I would sew for him oftener, but the other youth is rather cool and easy in his ways,— one of the lords of creation who consider it perfectly right and natural to have us wait on them, and I don't think it is worth while to make my services too common.

We are carrying out some jolly plans for Christmas. Amy called me into her state-room a few days ago and shut the door with an air of mystery. She then proposed that we should make Christmas presents for the three young men, and hang up their stockings on Christmas Eve, filled with whatever we could manufacture within a fortnight. Her capacious rag-bag furnishes stores of silk and ribbon for neckties, and we make many other things of which I will give you a list when they are completed. Of course we have to retire from public life while we are working, and for an hour or two every day I go into Amy's room and sit on the floor with her, planning, sewing and having lots of fun, greatly to the captain's mystification. He declares we are plotting something, perhaps a mutiny against him because he doesn't fully gratify our incessant craving for olives and sardines.

On the ninth of this month we passed the mouth of the Rio de la Plata, and encountered a severe storm with thunder and lightning. I woke up in the night hearing the deep rumble of thunder, but saw no lightning, for some one had thoughtfully closed the heavy wooden shutter outside my window. A stream of water was trickling down the wall into my berth from a leaky place in the deck overhead, and at first I was rather non-plussed by such a novel experience; then remembering that my mattress was too narrow for my berth, and consequently there was a nice little gutter for the rain to flow into, I resigned myself to slumber, trusting that the water would not collect fast enough to float me out into the cabin before morning.

That storm was the introduction to a change in our circumstances and mode of life. Cool, bracing weather, and bean-bag exercises, and brisk walks on deck take the place of quiet hours under our awning, yet sometimes we can sit up on the house, or on the "bitts" (wooden posts near the wheel) with warm wraps, watching the ocean's increased excitement as it comes near the ends of the earth. At these times a verse of Celia Thaxter's always comes into my head:

"Those splendid breakers! How they rushed,
   All emerald green and flashing white,
  Tumultuous in the morning sun
    With cheer and sparkle, and delight!"

December 29th.

I've *such* things to tell you now, Gussie! Experiences really worth ink and paper are these which have come to us since I wrote last in this journal. First let me tell you what happened on December twentieth, the day before we passed the Horn.

Early in the morning, Nora, the stewardess, came to tell me that land was in sight, and going on deck I saw mountains several miles away, and, what was almost as interesting to us, a barque. As the sea was calm, the captain had one of his boats made ready, and sent Mr. Duncan and the boatswain to board her, carrying a bag of buckwheat, New York papers (only two months old), and a bundle of tracts as a present to her captain. I was half wild with desire to go too, and so was Amy, but Arthur thought it would be difficult for us to do the climbing necessary to such an undertaking, and I agreed with him when I saw them swing themselves over the ship's side by a rope. Although there were no waves at all that day, the great ocean-swells would sometimes almost hide the little boat, as we watched it rather anxiously. It reached the barque after less than an hour's pull, and they brought back from her captain a box of fine raisins. She was on her way from Malaga to San Francisco. In the afternoon we caught up with her, and sailed so near that the two captains shouted a conversation back and forth. Arthur said to us: "Now, girls, put on your scarlet jackets, so they can see more plainly that I have ladies on board the 'Lyra.' I want them to know what a happy man I am."

It was queer to be so near a little company of strangers far at sea, and they stared at us and we returned the compliment as if the queerness was fully appreciated on both sides. Before we were out of their sight the "Lyra's" bean-bag club (*i. e.* Amy, Mr. Fordyce and I) felt the need of doing something to keep warm, and began to toss the bags about. Mr. F. said he had no doubt that the lonely captain and officers of the barque were watching our fun with envious eyes, and wishing they had some young lady passengers to enliven their monotony. Generally, we play with great precision and skill, but that evening we felt rather wild, I think, and carried on a disorderly warfare, the chief aim of which seemed to be the heaving of two bags at once against some unhappy being. Mr. Fordyce unintentionally sent one at my "starboard eye" with such force that for a moment I feared it would be my sad fate to go through the rest of my life with only one.

Later in the evening we took a long walk on the main deck with Arthur. I think we must have walked three miles altogether, for we kept it up from nine to eleven not caring to go in while rosy sunset streaks remained in the sky, and at last we grew too sleepy to wait any longer for darkness to come. These Antarctic evenings are strangely fascinating. Think of our reading large print by twilight at ten o'clock P. M., in December, when you at home have had the gas lighted for five hours.

The next morning, December twenty-first, we entered the straits of Le Maire. I looked out of the cabin window with a vague idea that there might be land in view, and saw mountains rising out of the sea, apparently very near. That was a startling sight for eyes grown accustomed to the vast watery plain, and we rushed on deck to look through the marine glass at the constantly changing view. We were favored with a fair wind, and sped through the straits at the rate of thirteen knots an hour, so that when I had provided myself with paper and pencil, hoping to get some poor memento of the scene, the rapid changes in the landscape . made me almost despair, while with numb fingers I worked laboriously, every moment resolving to lay down my pencil and enjoy Nature to the utmost, without trying to reproduce it on paper. It was not until my paper was covered, though, and the white rail by which I stood disfigured with scrawls that I gave myself up to full enjoyment of the mountains.

The weather was chilly, and the sky rather cloudy, especially in the direction of Staten Land on our left, which we could only see indistinctly looming up behind the fog, but the coast of Tierra del Fuego on the opposite side was not more than three miles away.

As we went through the straits, mountain after mountain came into view, of all shapes and sizes, a continuous line: their prevailing character bare and rugged, being almost destitute of trees, and sprinkled with snow-patches around their tops, but some had a greenish hue, as if covered with moss. How lonely they looked as we sailed by them! Water-fowl rising in flocks from the sea were the only signs of life among those solitudes.

After dinner the land was in the distance, and I stayed on deck only long enough to see how we were beating a whaler, and catching up with an iron English ship, which we soon left far behind, greatly to Captain Roslyn's exultation.

At eight o'clock he called us to come directly on deck to see the celebrated Cape Horn; so, well protected against the rain with water-proofs, we went up to see what will make that evening one to be remembered for a life-time.

Not far off was a bleak line of coast, with curious groups of rocks in the water near it; the farthest point in the line a pyramidal rock, much higher than the rest. That was Cape Horn, and we were sailing quietly where I thought tempests always raged. It looked lofty, as we came near enough to see the streaks of lichens or seaweed on its black, barren sides, and when the "Lyra" sailed abreast of it, I thought it was almost high enough to be called a mountain. There was grandeur in that picture of utter desolation, and it seemed the most natural thing in the world for us to burst out as we did in the doxology, "Praise God from whom all blessings flow," for there we were, literally at the land's end, our great ship like an egg-shell compared with the mighty deep around and beneath us, and we had been led from our homes and preserved amid many dangers by our Father's hand. I wondered if Cape Horn echoes were ever roused by a doxology before.

Arthur's voice behind me said, as if to himself: "All the ends of the earth shall see the salvation of our God."

We were two hours in passing Horn Island, and though it was broad daylight till ten, the rain began to fall so heavily that we felt obliged to go down, after a parting look at the dark sentinel of the continent, half-shrouded in mist. By the cabin-stove we warmed ourselves, saying: "Is it possible that we are past Cape Horn; that place so feared and dreaded by us since we sailed!" and all agreed that the evening's pleasures had not been surpassed even by those of moonlight in the tropics.

The day before Christmas was the roughest we have ever known, and I am grateful that we survived it without any broken bones; yet there was fun in it, as we were not at all seasick. It is not exactly convenient, I can assure you, when standing before the glass arranging my locks, to be kept in perpetual motion, hurled from my position, and dashed against the door with brush in hand, then back to the glass again, but it entirely prevents unnecessary prinking, and is, no doubt, good for my character, even if it does make me late for breakfast.

The important business of filling the stockings had to be attended to on the twenty-fourth, in spite of all such inconveniences as those I have mentioned, and many of the presents being too large to go into a stocking, had to be hung on the outside. The book of "Familiar Quotations" was brought into use to supply mottoes for some articles which were put in more as jokes than gifts. The hosiery we had to steal from the captain, of course, and as he has unusually small feet for a man, the stockings were not so capacious as we could have wished. By the way, I must tell you of Nora's astonishment at Captain Roslyn's shoes, which she saw when she was "fixing up of his room one day; and, Miss

Amy, child, I says to myself: 'How can a man with such small feet have any constitution to learn anything!'" Amy said she supposed Nora must have thought that his *understanding* was limited.

Excuse this disgression from the important matter in the foreground. We gave our captain two neckties, a shoe-case made of duck (which we inveigled Mr. Fordyce into getting for us, out of the ship's stores), and bound with scarlet braid; an illuminated text, painted by Miss Marion Gilmer, under the greatest difficulties, and a pen-wiper; also a pin-ball shaped like a flying-fish, the scales marked in ink, and a row of pins ornamenting his dorsal fin. This article was made in reference to some joke of ours about a dead flying-fish which an unseen hand propelled through Amy's window one day.

The stocking destined for Mr. Duncan contained a shoe-case like the captain's, a necktie, a lace bag full of lumps of sugar, and labelled "Cape Horn confectionery," and a pin-cushion.

But Mr. Fordyce's stocking was a triumph of art and genius. Amy made him a brush and comb case, resplendent with pink bows, and I a brown silk necktie. We also presented him with a bottle of lemon syrup (stolen, I grieve to say, from the pantry, but the theft was afterwards confessed, and pardoned), and a tiny bean-bag as a reminiscence of our club, with B. B. C. printed on it, and the written motto attached, was: "Let all your aims be high,"— a gentle reminder for him to avoid throwing his bag at my eyes in future. A hideous pen-and-ink sketch of Poe's Raven, "sitting on the bust of Pallas," was the last of our favors toward this undeserving youth.

We had to sit up late on Christmas Eve, in order to hang the loaded stockings on the door handles without fear of discovery, and the motion of the vessel caused us to stagger about the dark cabin as if intoxicated, until they were safely suspended, and then we went to our respective rooms, after a loving embrace and mutual congratulations upon the success of our undertaking, and were lulled to sleep by a Cape Horn breeze sighing and shrieking through our windows.

Great was the excitement the next morning over the visit of Santa Claus, and we found he had not forgotten us; a jar of pickles being tied by a cord to Amy's door handle, and one of olives to mine, with the sentiment: "Olive forever."

Arthur said Mr. Duncan had come to him in high glee, reporting the appendage on his door, and Mr. Fordyce appeared after breakfast with my necktie on, Amy's brush and comb-case slung on his back like a knapsack, the bottle of syrup stuffed into his breast pocket, and the likeness of the "Raven" in his hat band, to make grateful acknowledgments of the young ladies' kindness. Captain Arthur did not discover his flying-fish, and we, suspecting as much from the absence of allusion to what we considered our *chef d' œuvre*, found it in the toe of his stocking, and set him off into fits of laughter when we showed it to him.

January 5th.

I ought not to write another word in this joint letter, having already gone beyond due limits; but never mind, Gussie, for I really must tell you about the close of the old year, and opening of the new one.

On the last afternoon of 18 —, we attempted a candy scrape, whereof the molasses wouldn't boil as it was expected to, and we tried hard to relish a mixture of sour molasses and nuts, eaten with spoons, but it took a deal of imagining to make us believe we were eating candy.

Amy and I resolved to see the year out, and at a few minutes before twelve, we went on deck. There, in the quiet starlight, we welcomed 18—, and thoughts of past and future made me feel unusually reflective. Just as the "for'ard" bell gave eight strokes for midnight, a great din arose in that part of the ship among the sailors, who rang the bell violently, drummed on tin pans, shouted and exchanged New Year's greetings, while above all rose the voice of the boatswain singing his favorite melody: "Shall we gather at the river?" All this took away much of the solemnity of the time, for though I was ready to welcome the new year with a song of praise in my heart, such riotous proceedings were hardly in accordance with my feelings.

Like two silly girls, as we doubtless are, we took it into our heads to stay on deck for a few hours and see the sun rise, but were beginning to shiver in our seats on the "bitts," when Mr. Duncan asked us if we could trust him to make us very comfortable, which he did by spreading shawls and cushions on the deck, and wrapping us up as if for a sleighride, in a warm rug of his own. Then he sat by us on the sky-light, and we had a delightful talk, learning to know and respect our usually reserved first officer more than ever, as he told us what we had only gathered before from scraps of conversation — of his early life in the West, where he struggled hard to conquer his love of the sea, for he knew his duty was to remain upon his widowed mother's farm, and it was not easy to throw all his energies into work that he hated, yet he did it for three years; then his mother was relieved by second marriage from fear of poverty, and he left free to be led by his own preferences. His aim in life, he said, is to be a faithful Christian captain, like Arthur, a kind of sailors' missionary, and to take with him on his voyages a little sister, now in a boarding school, whose delicate health causes him some anxiety, for she is the only one living in whom he can feel the right of possession.

We talked on all sorts of subjects grave and

gay, and speculated on the strange foreign scenes through which the new year might lead us. The starlight was beautiful, but at three o'clock, just as a faint light was dawning in the east, a bank of clouds from the horizon mounted up and spread a dull grey curtain over the whole sky. Our chance of seeing any sunrise was gone, and I began to feel rather blue, for this dawn of 18—, was not enlivening. More chilly and stiff than romantic, were the girls who crept down to their staterooms, and all day we were so stupidly sleepy as to excite Arthur's wonderment that merely sitting up till midnight should have had such an effect upon us. At last we exposed all our folly, and were well laughed at for our pains.

Now, I really am not going to write any more in this journal till we get to San Francisco, except to tell you that it would rejoice your heart to see how well and happy Amy is looking. She seems as strong as I am now, (such a contrast to what she was six months ago, when I thought we were going to lose her!) and has such high spirits that I sometimes look at her in amazement, asking myself: "Can this be my Amy?" That serene, pale face of hers, that we both love so well, is flushed like the inside of a sea-shell by the rough winds of the Cape, and her brown eyes sparkle with life and gaiety all the time. This voyage is a success so far, certainly, in doing her good, and as for me, I was well enough before I left home, and now I am growing so fat on duff, baked beans, and "salt horse," that Arthur makes me the subject of his frequent merriment, declaring that my face resembles the reddest side of a russet apple.

You will think I have not acquired the art of leaving off, whatever may be my other accomplishments, so I will say good-by, my dear old girl, hoping that you are not entirely out of patience with

    Your loving   MARION.

CHAPTER III.

SAN FRANCISCO.

AMY'S STORY.

*February 12th, 18 —,
At Anchor in San Francisco Bay.*

OUR voyage of one hundred and ten days came to an end this morning; but as we do not go up to the wharf till evening, I can add a few closing words to you, my dear.

All our friends when they read in the Boston *Transcript* to-morrow: "Ship 'Lyra' Captain Roslyn, arr'd, at San Francisco, after a passage of one hundred and ten days," will say with great relief: "Those poor girls were n't drowned off the Horn after all, then! How glad they will be to set foot on dry land!" It is true that I am deeply grateful for the way in which we have been led through the perils of the sea to the western coast of our native country, yet there is such happiness in a sea-life, that I am loth to exchange it for the bustle of a city, even for a while.

On the evening of the eleventh, the captain told us that at ten o'clock, or soon after, we should see Farralone Light outside the Golden Gate, and we on deck in the damp darkness shivered with cold and excitement, while straining our eyes to catch a glimpse of the distant spark. It was not more than twenty minutes past ten when from the mast-head a sailor cried: "Light, ho!" The accuracy of calculation by which a captain, after sailing thousands of miles, could predict within half an hour the time when a light should appear, made me respect the science of navigation.

Just at sunrise we went through the Golden Gate, and gazed with rapture at the verdant hills that guard the entrance to San Francisco's great harbor, among whose vessels the "Lyra" sailed proudly, and dropped her anchor at last with a vibrating ring of the great iron chain that seemed like an exultant "amen" to a prosperous voyage.

There are friends in the city to whose house we shall go to-night,— the Wildings; friends as yet unseen by us, (with one exception), but long known by reputation. Mr. Wilding and my father were close comrades in their boyhood, and in their early manhood studied law in the same office. Then the former went to San Francisco and settled there, and when father died he wrote Arthur a letter of most affectionate sympathy, saying that if ever he could render any service to Herbert Roslyn's children for the sake of his love to their father, nothing would gratify him more. Therefore, when Arthur first thought of taking Marion and myself on a voyage he wrote to Mr. Wilding that we should hope to see him in California some time in the month of February, and an answer soon came with a cordial invitation for us to make his house our home as long as we could remain in San Francisco.

This answer only came a few days before we sailed, and I did not think of telling you about it, for was not a long experience of ocean life between ourselves and the kind welcome awaiting us on the Pacific coast, causing it to seem very distant and unreal? Now, it is a pleasant reality, and Mr. Wilding's son came on board this morning soon after we anchored, to assure us of it. To tell the truth, in the excitement of our arrival, I had almost forgotten that there were any such people as the Wildings, when I suddenly espied a stout young man with a brown moustache shaking hands with Marion, to whom the captain had just presented him, and bidding her welcome to San Francisco with the cordiality of an old acquaintance. He brought us our letters, which had been sent to his father's care, and we were so anxious to hear from all our friends at home, that we were not very polite to him, I'm afraid. He considerately took himself off, promising to return at tea-time in the steam-tug which is to convey us to the wharf, and we were at liberty to read the news. So many letters and everybody alive and well! What cause for thanksgiving we have! Your letter of forty pages absorbed our united attention for an hour, during which time we forgot where we were, and lived through the winter with you; going to lectures, symphony concerts, oratorios, painting-class, sewing-schools and tenement houses where your poor friends congregate. You have lived a more useful life lately than that of your sea-faring friends; but perhaps they have laid up health and glad memories that will make them better workers for others in days to come. We will hope so.

I am sorry we missed the grand wedding of the season,—Sophie Moore's,—and Marion is especially so, for she remembers making mud-pies with her when they were next-door neighbors in K—— street, and says they "used to fight like two cats." Such memories would add interest to a wedding ceremony.

I must close this letter and mail it when we land, which I almost dread to do. Can you believe that, after nearly four months at sea? A congenial company have been the captain, officers and passengers of the "Lyra," and who can tell if we shall all sail again together from this port? Mr. Duncan will take command of a ship if he can find one here, I suppose, and if Mr. Fordyce gets a summons from his home he will go there by rail; but I trust these "ifs" will not become stern facts to break up the "Lyra's" pleasant circle. I hear the shrill whistle of the steam-tug, and we must get ready to go ashore. Already we have donned costumes that are suitable to an appearance in city streets, and the brown faces reflected in the glass certainly harmonize better with our sea-dresses of soft, dark flannel, than with these light grey ruffles and loopings. Marion fears the Wildings will take us for descendants of the Digger Indians.

We will write more by and by, but not quite such a volume as this, which now closes, with love from both your friends,

AMY ROSLYN.
MARION GILMER.

San Francisco, March 12*th*, 18—.

DEAR GUSSIE,— A long drive to-day has left me rather too tired this evening to accompany Marion and the others to a concert, and the rarity of such quiet hours as this one, induces me to make the most of my time in writing to you.

If Marion and I had been two long-absent daughters of the Wilding family, they could hardly have given us a heartier welcome when we came from the "Lyra" to more spacious quarters in this elegant mansion. Western people know how to make their guests feel at home, without doubt; stiffness and formality are unknown to them, if I may judge from my short acquaintance with San Franciscans, and we know more people now, after being here three weeks, than Mrs. Grantly, our hostess, would know after a three months' visit with us in Boston, I am convinced; for their free and easy ways, if they do sometimes astonish a stranger, have a tendency to make the most reserved person descend from stateliness, and meet them half-way.

Mrs. Grantly is a young widow,— Mr. Wildding's only daughter,— a tiny creature with wavy hair, and eyes that remind me of a kitten's in their expression,— roguishness and innocence being so singularly combined.

Mrs. Wilding died years ago, and the head of the family is a man whose genial nature is expressed by every look and tone. His eldest son, Robert, our first San Francisco acquaintance, devotes himself to us as if he had no other object in life than to see that our impressions of this city are of the most favorable kind, and from morning to midnight he would escort us up and down these hilly streets, if our strength was equal to his good-nature.

The only member of the family whom I have not yet described is "Jim," the youngest son. He is a *real boy*, aged thirteen, and you can easily form your opinion of him from these particulars. Of course he is Marion's faithful knight,— boys of his age always are, in return for her undisguised interest in them.

So much for the family. As to the city, I like it in spite of its steep hills, and the scarcity of trees. There is some quality in the air that causes such an effervescence of my spirits that I am in a mood to be pleased with everything.

Only think of calla lilies lifting their creamy heads by hundreds in yards that separate the houses only a few feet from the sidewalks! and across the bay in Alameda there is the rich verdure of our June grass, blossoming fruit trees, and a wilderness of ivies and flowers about the houses, although the weather is cool enough to remind us of autumn forests, rather than of spring gardens. We spent a day or two there with some pleasant people, and drove over to Oakland, also gay with young green leaves and flowers. A lady with whom we took lunch gave me a little century plant, which I shall carry with me on my future travels in memory of the freshness and joy of that spring day; however the others may laugh at me for setting my affections on a thing so devoid of any "soft, attractive grace."

To-day Robert Wilding drove his sister, Marion, and myself, out to the Cliff House, where we sat on the piazza and surveyed the wide Pacific, rolling almost from our feet far out beyond the Golden Gate. Most people are interested in watching the slimy-looking seals that bob their round heads out of the water, and swarm over the rocks near the hotel; but I did not appreciate them, for the sight of the ocean makes me oblivious to everything else. For once, though, I was willing to turn from it to look at the beautiful green hills through which our onward road wound. They were bright with red, yellow, and blue flowers,— not hiding shyly among the grass and brushes like our fringed gentians, or the trailing arbutus, but each one large and erect, nodding its gay head to us as the breeze swept by, and the hills looked as if they were covered with variegated carpets.

I turned back and saw between them a blue strip of sea; then my forward gaze met a grand view of the city and harbor of San Francisco, as we suddenly came around the shoulder of a hill. In one of the quiet lanes we left the horses tied to a fence, and spreading the carriage robes in a verdant field, camped out among the scarlet poppies to eat our lunch. I remembered while sitting there that on the twelfth of March one year ago I was very ill with diphtheretic sore throat, and outside the house snow and ice prevailed with bitter winds. To-day, with health restored, the happy memory of one hundred and ten days of sea-life behind me, and a prospect of much good in store, I thought "Truly, 'He maketh me to lie down in green pastures,' and 'What shall I render unto the Lord for all His benefits toward me?'" In all hours of life that are marked by a peculiar depth of any experience, either of sorrow or joy, how the Bible words come into the minds of those who love them as the truest expression of their feelings! We do not find it so with uninspired words.

You ask in your last letter if we have seen much of the Chinese element in San Francisco. We have seen numbers of Chinamen in the streets, but knowing that the "Lyra's" bow will soon be pointed toward the Celestial Empire, we thought it would be better to receive our first impressions of the idolatries and the social life of the heathen in their own country.

Many churches here have Chinese Sunday-schools connected with them, and it is interesting to see the scholars with their loose blue sacks and long queues, listening to some bright young girl, or thoughtful man, as they try to show them the way of Life.

It surprises me to find how the people in San Francisco interest themselves in the vessels that come here. One of them that is remarkable for anything,— speed or handsome cabins, for instance,— is sure to be visited by crowds; and several times when Marion and I have gone down to the "Lyra" with friends to whom we wished to exhibit "our home" (as we really feel it to be), we have encountered curious strangers prying about the cabins, and evidently regretting that our state-rooms were locked, which we considered a matter for self-congratulation.

One afternoon we took a long walk with Robert Wilding and Mr. Fordyce, and decided for novelty's sake to take tea on board the ship, and go to a lecture afterward on our way back to Mr. Wilding's house. The sound of pouring rain on the cabin roof assured us that we had no need to anticipate the lecture, and might as well make up our minds not to leave the ship before morning. The captain came in, and finding us as composedly settled as if we were on a long voyage, instead of being moored to Vallejo street wharf, looked somewhat astonished, but laughingly bade us welcome to his ship, and proceeded to make himself as comfortable as we were.

He had two pieces of news to impart, and, after teasing us a long time, announced that we were to take a passenger to the Sandwich Islands on our way to China, and we *may* be able to make a visit of a few days at

Honolulu. Our delight was great at this unexpected addition to the list of foreign ports at which we were hoping to touch in the course of our voyage; but a passenger! — that would be a doubtful blessing. Some disagreeable person, perhaps, to break up our harmonious party.

"Now, don't borrow trouble, girls," said the captain, "before you know whether he *is*. disagreeable, or the concentration of all manly virtues. 'A young man?' Yes, Marion, he is rather young; about the age of your respected cousin, the captain of the 'Lyra.' 'Where am I going to put him?' In the state-room opposite Amy's, of course."

"But that is our store-room!"

"I should judge so," said Arthur, opening the door, and taking an inventory of its contents. "Rag-bags, magazines, waterproof cloaks, guitar-case, old hats and boots lying about promiscuously! This place has got to be fitted up for Mr. Lewis Curran's state-room, although chaos reigns here now; and, by the way, he must be two inches longer than this berth. What shall I do about that?"

"Cut a hole in the wall at the end of it for each foot, and let him extend them into the pantry," suggested Mr. Fordyce.

"When are we going to see the creature?" asked Marion.

"We will give a party down here on the ship when the moon is full, and ask every one of our San Francisco friends to be present. Mr. Curran can come too, and see how he likes his accommodations and his fellow-passengers."

Arthur's plan met with approval, and we proceeded to write a list of those who were to be favored with an invitation to this novel entertainment,— a moonlight party at Vallejo street wharf. I will keep my letter for a few days, and let you know how it passed off.

March 16th.

The moonlight last night was all we could wish, and soon after a six o'clock dinner, Marion and I started for the wharf, with Mrs. Grantly, Robert and Jim. A small crowd of friends came trooping over the gangway, half an hour later, and we had a very funny, informal kind of a party. In the lighted cabins our guests amused themselves with music and photograph albums, or inspected our pretty state-rooms, and wished it had been their happy lot to go on a long voyage in such a ship as the "Lyra." On deck, romantic couples paced up and down, or sat in the bows, looking over the harbor, whose fleet of anchored vessels, as well as the surrounding hills were brought into soft distinctness by the flood of moonlight; and a party of seven mounted the "spanker-boom" and sat there, making the night vocal.

Marion was enjoying herself upon this elevated perch, when she saw a solitary figure ascend the gangway steps, and she sprang down to tell me that "the passenger," that much dreaded character, was coming on board.

Robert Wilding and Mr. Fordyce were with us when Arthur advanced with a very tall young man, whom he introduced as "Mr. Curran, our fellow-passenger."

We had just enough uncomfortable consciousness of the remarks passed two nights before upon this gentleman, to make us exceedingly stiff in responding to the introduction, and some time after the captain called me to account for it, begging me not to act as if I grudged him a fortnight's passage on our ship. Therefore I expressed contrition, and took pains to be pleasant to Mr. Curran when I found a minute to speak to him. He had met our stiffness with an equal amount of the same; but when I tried to make amends for our share of it, he unbent, and we had a friendly chat until supper was announced.

Now San Franciscans know what good living is, and I was well aware that ship cookery needs sea appetites; accordingly I sat down to our loaded table with a heart full of misgivings. The supper looked as if it were good, the people seemed hungry, and my courage revived, until, glancing at Marion, I met her eyes fixed on me with a look that said unutterable things. "If anything is wrong, it must be the crab-salad," I thought, a cold perspiration coming out upon my brow as I watched the faces of those who helped themselves to that delicacy, and noticed that no one took more than two mouthfuls, and that the first one caused a look of surprise, the second of disgust. At last I ventured to taste it myself. My first impulse was to exclaim: "kerosene!" for there was a strong flavor of something entirely foreign to the usual ingredients of salad, and it seemed as much like that as anything. Persevering until six mouthfuls were dispatched, I found the flavor was of raw onions, and slightly rancid oil. Mr. Curran was watching me, and as I met his amused glance we both laughed so much that it was half a minute before I could regain my voice to tell him that there was yet time for him to give up his passage on the "Lyra," if he feared a frequent repetition of onion salad during his voyage to Honolulu.

Some of our guests went home directly after supper, and the rest of them, with ourselves, left the ship a little before midnight, every one saying: "How much more fun this has been than any commonplace drawing-room party!"

In a few days we sail, and Mr. Duncan still retains his post of first officer, for he did not find in San Francisco any vessel that he could take command of, and he told me he had not taken a great deal of pains, being very well satisfied at present where he is.

This is my last letter until we send our mail from Honolulu.

Ever yours, lovingly, AMY.

CHAPTER IV.

CROSSING THE PACIFIC.

MARION'S STORY.

Ship "Lyra," Pacific Ocean,
April 6th, 18—.

DEAR GUSSIE,— Our ship is speeding toward the Hawaiian islands, but she bears a third less of me than she did when we came to the shores of California. The missing third remains in that blissful country, and never did it cause me such a wrench of my feelings to leave any place. Leaving home was nothing to it, for then "the world was all before me, where to choose," and the prospect of seeing it sustained me; but I sailed from San Francisco with a settled conviction that never more, in heathen or Christian lands, should I be likely to have such a good time as I had there.

The day before we sailed, the "Lyra" left the wharf and anchored a little way down the harbor, where we had to go out to her in a row-boat. That dear boy, Jim, went with us to enliven me to the last possible moment. He and his brother Robert spent the night on board, making, with Mr. Curran, the officers, Arthur, Amy and myself, quite an array at the tea-table, and we were not a funereal party, although I am sure that to more than half of our number an often recurring thought of the next morning's sailing came somewhat like the shadow of the guillotine upon the merry-making of the prisoners, who tried to forget what their morrow would surely bring. Every one was so kind to us in San Francisco that it was hard to say good-bye, knowing that we are not likely to see any of them again for years, if ever; and as you have heard me long for a brother just a few years younger than myself, you can understand my regret when, having found Jim Wilding the exact pattern after which I should cut one out if it were possible, I had to see him borne from me by a cruel steam-tug, which carried out of our sight about thirty esteemed friends. They came off in the tug, these cordial souls, to do us honor, and enjoy a sail down the harbor, as the tug went ahead about a hundred feet, drawing the ship after her by a long hawser, and we stood in the bows to be as near them as possible.

The sky became overcast, and the water so rough that it was not easy for us to stand where we did, heartlessly laughing at the suffering of the passengers on the little tug, which had begun to toss about like a shuttle-cock. I didn't feel merry, but that sight was too much for me. A dozen ladies were kneeling in a row by the rail, gazing intently, with pallid countenances, upon the cold, gray waves, and the anguish of their expressions made me sure they were saying to their inmost souls: "Oh! why did this wretched 'Lyra' ever come to San Francisco to bring us into such misery?" And they were on a pleasure party! I was justly rewarded for laughing at them, for soon the steam-tug drew in her rope from us, and turned back, the gentlemen giving shouts of farewell, and some of the ladies, who were not wholly incapacitated, feebly waving their handkerchiefs; and before I had watched them quite out of sight, I began to feel "kind of funny," as our stewardesss says when she is mildly seasick, and sought my state-room, only stopping a moment to speak a few words of cheer to our new passenger, who was sitting on the hatchway, with the dejected expression of one who is in the iron grip of homesickness. I do not mean Mr. Curran; didn't you know we had *two* new passengers? The second one is Jim's yellow cat, the darling of his heart, which he insisted on giving me as a parting gift, or "legacy," he said, to help me always to remember him. I realized the preciousness of the gift, and couldn't bear to deprive the boy of his "Yaller," as he euphoniously calls her, and only consented to take her when I saw two bright hazel eyes grow dim at my refusal. With her natural charms embellished by a lavender neck-ribbon, "Yaller" became one of the "Lyra's" passengers, but whether she has gone down into the hold to indulge in silent melancholy, or has become a victim to Neptune, I cannot discover, for ever since our first day out, when she seemed terrified at the heaving of the cabin floor, we have seen no trace of her but her blonde hairs scattered over the green sofa cushions.

On that first day I sought my berth, and lay there until evening, less affected by sea-sickness than by low spirits, and a weariness quite natural after six weeks of sight-seeing, company, and late hours. Before tea I aroused from my lethargy, and went to inquire after Amy's condition. She was "*in medias res*," her misery being such that even I could do her no greater favor than to let her alone, and I despondently went upon deck, half-dreading to see the dull, gray ocean that was just separating me from the land of my affection.

Hearty welcomes greeted me from the captain and Mr. Duncan. "Where have you been all this time, little girl?" said the former; "not seasick, surely?"

"Suffering from *mal de la terre*, if there is such a thing, much more than *mal de mer*," I answered, listlessly. "The sea does not seem as beautiful to me now as it did six months ago. How dark and dreary it is!"

"You are looking in the wrong quarter, Miss Marion," said Mr. Duncan. "Turn around to the west." There I saw a broad band of orange sky, and waves tinged with a bronze light; a bracing wind blew my hat off, and my dolefulness went with it. How much good it does to look in the right direction when we have the blues! (A moral reflection that you will do well to remember, Gussie.) After all, I had as much to be thankful for as ever; the same pleasant company as on our last voyage, with the addition of an intelligent young lawyer and a yellow cat from San Francisco, and what *was* I moping about?

A strain of music from the forecastle made us aware that one of our new sailors possesses a concertina, and knows how to play on it very nicely. "Love among the roses," was the air he gave us then, and Mr. Curran felt some secret chord thrilled by the familiar strain, I think, for he went to the taffrail and leaned upon it, gazing in the direction of land. It was my duty to try if I could cheer him a little, I suppose, but I was rather afraid of him; perhaps because he treated me as if he considered me very young, and a scatter-brained individual into the bargain. It is depressing to know that any one has a bad opinion of you, and for a while I was nearly as stiff with him as in the hour of our introduction.

The next day was dark, and the vessel rolled, and creaked her timbers in a way that made me feel vicious. Amy was in her stateroom, from which all my persuasions were of no avail to bring her out, and after fairly tipping over in a low, easy chair, when a prolonged roll dislodged all movable things, I climbed into my berth, as the only secure place, and sat curled up there like a kitten in a hay-loft. The window of my state-room is on a level with the berth, and when sitting close to it, as I was then, every word of mine could be overheard by those on the starboard side of the deck, but I didn't take that into consideration as I opened "Paradise Lost," and began to commit to memory a part of Satan's address to Beelzebub, for a few fragments of it had been wandering in the dusty corners of my brain, and I knew the only way to drive them out was to learn the lines connectedly. Therefore, just imagine the absurdity of my exclaiming in our revered preceptor's own manner: "If thou be'est he! But oh, how fallen, how changed!" and "Fallen cherub, to be weak is miserable, doing or suffering," etc., and of hearing, when I paused, the voice of Mr. Curran saying in a low tone: "What can she be talking about, Fordyce? Lamenting a change in some friend, it appears. Has she left her heart in San Francisco, I wonder?"

Indignation made me as stony as if I had had a vision of the Gorgon's head with snaky locks, and my book dropped from my hand over the side of the berth, hearing which, the young men had the manners to move off and finish their remarks at a safe distance.

At dinner I made some mischievous allusion to the ease with which conversation on deck could be heard in the state-rooms, and had the gratification of seeing Mr. Curran change countenance, and regard me with an inquiring look, as if seeking an explanation, which we had afterward with a good deal of fun, and we soon found ourselves on a more sociable footing.

Amy gave us her ever-welcome presence before night, for seasickness had fled, leaving her weak and pale, but even more than usually bright, and she checkmated our passenger in a deep game of chess during the evening while I sat by them with my attention riveted upon the board. After this mental combat they felt the need of refreshment, and we opened a great box of candy, a gift from Robert Wilding, and took it into the forward cabin to treat the officers. There must have been six pounds of the choicest candy in that box, but there is not a crumb left now, after about ten conferences held over it by us all since it was opened. Every night we have placed the box in the centre of the dining-room table, and all knelt around it on the settees, discussing the merits of its contents, and each one fixing an eye upon the pieces of candy he or she desired,— then five hands made a sudden grab, and the captain bore off the precious box to its locker, proclaiming the candy conference adjourned till the next night.

There has been a good deal of unpleasant weather since we sailed, and the idea of arriving so soon at Honolulu makes me feel quite unsettled, as if it were not worth while to start on any of our old routines of reading and study. On damp evenings very good concerts have been held in the "Lyra's" cabin, for Mr. Curran is a fine performer upon the flute, and plays duets with Arthur, or else he gives us a flute solo with an organ accompaniment by Amy, and when clear skies make it pleasant for us to be on deck, we have vocal music there, with the guitar. We shall be sorry on this account to leave Mr. Curran at Honolulu, and he has really been an agreeable addition to our party during the short time we have sailed together. I don't know how well he would wear on a long voyage. To any one who wants to choose a friend—as the Vicar of Wakefield's wife chose her wedding gown—"for qualities that wear well," I can recommend our first mate, and one is always sure of finding him just the same, never brilliant, and never dull.

There has been only one moonlight evening thus far on our passage, and that was so beautiful that all the sailors, as well as the passengers, were out till past midnight enjoying themselves. It is comical to see what grown men will do to amuse themselves on a ship! Finding Mr. Curran's talk on civil and common law too prosaic for such an evening, I wandered away from the group on the house, and looked down on the main deck to see how the sailors were passing the time, for a clattering of something on a tin pan, and frequent bursts of laughter aroused my curiosity. One of the men had a wooden Jim Crow, whose movable joints were fastened by rivets made out of our hairpins, as I was informed afterwards, and he was dancing it on a pan for the general entertainment.

In two days these feet of mine, that have trodden the paths of learning in your company hundreds of times, will press Hawaiian soil! I shall recline under the spreading palms, eating "poi" with my forefinger from a cocoanut shell like a native Kanaka, and bananas will be so plenty that I shall think no more of them than if they were corn cobs. Imagine my bliss, then, if you can!

I think I will stop writing, for, on looking over these pages, I see there is neither wisdom nor profit in them, and being doubtful if I am likely to improve just now, my narrative shall be cut short, to be continued when I reach the shores of Asia.

Ever yours,   MARION.

Hawaiian Islands. — Page 91.

AMY'S STORY.

Pacific Ocean, May 2nd, 18 —.

This letter was to be made especially interesting to you, dear Gussie, by a full description of what we enjoyed in Honolulu, and as Marion and I did not go there after all, I fear you will read it with disappointment almost as great as that experienced by us, when the bright visions upon which we had been living for a fortnight proved hardly more substantial than a fading mirage.

Ah, well! it was one of the slips " 'twixt the cup and the lip" so common to all, and after the great mercies that have attended us, we must not be ungrateful enough to complain if one pleasure is withheld. Perhaps you will find some interest in an account of how we *did n't* visit Honolulu.

On the ninth of April we drew near to the Hawaiian group, seeing Molokai first of all in the distance; then we had a near view of Oahu, whose aspect was most forbidding, suggestive of volcanic fires, and our ideas of tropical beauty received a shock as we looked at it, but, rounding the corner of the island, there came in sight a landscape of surpassing loveliness. The town of Honolulu, with its white church spires, and houses shaded by rich foliage, is in a recess formed by the mountains, which curve around it almost to the water's edge. Many of them are extinct volcanoes, curiously shaped, and relieved from barrenness by a soft blending of green, brown, yellow and crimson hues. The soil in some places is so red that we thought the color was caused by fields of brilliant flowers, and with the beach of dazzling sand, the rows of cocoa-nut palms beyond it, and the translucent blue sea breaking upon it in a white fringe of foam, there were enough elements of beauty to form a rare picture.

The captain gave orders that the anchor should be dropped, and prepared to go on shore with Mr. Curran, telling us if he found there that he could obtain enough cargo for China to justify a few days' detention, he would come back for us, and let us spend every moment of the time in Honolulu. There was a slight shade of doubt cast upon us by Arthur's proviso, soon removed, however, for the pilot who boarded the vessel told him some commercial facts that made him turn back, as he was going down the gangway, to call out that we must be all ready to go ashore after dinner. Mr. Curran said he would be on the beach to welcome us, and went off, not even deeming it necessary to say farewell leaving us to pass several hours in a state of joyous expectancy, while we surveyed the picturesque town before us with the marine glass, by help of which equestrians on the beach could be plainly seen; and we planned a horse-back ride for ourselves at sunrise the next day.

With the afternoon came a gathering cloud of misgivings. The wind had risen and there were two miles of rough water between the "Lyra's" girls and the land they longed to visit. A coral reef, over which the waves were tossing up foam, must be passed in a little boat, and we anxiously watched one that was pushed off from the beach and rowed toward us, for it danced about in a way that made me tremble at the thought of returning in it.

"Why! Arthur isn't there," Marion cried at last. "There is only a crew of half-clothed heathen."

"The Sandwich Islanders are not heathen;" I suggested, but when the boat was near, I hoped that the real heathen would not appear more outlandish than the dark-skinned men who rowed it. They brought a note from Arthur.

"DEAR GIRLS,— No cargo worth waiting for. I should be unfaithful to the owners were I to detain the ship for our own gratification, so we sail to-night at ten. This boat will bring back Mr. Curran's luggage, and if the sea grows smoother by three o'clock, you may come on shore and spend a few hours. I would have sent Mr. Fordyce to the ship as an escort for you if I could have spared him from my business here; but you need n't fear the natives, they are not as wild as they look."

With the blankest disappointment we looked at each other — at the boat heavily weighted with trunks, and noticed several inches of water in it, — at the sea which had grown rougher since Arthur wrote his letter — and we pondered. Mr. Duncan could not leave the ship in her captain's absence, and I hope the Kanakas will pardon me if I do them injustice in saying that, to my unaccustomed eyes, they appeared almost uncivilized enough to have killed and eaten us on our way to their island. Moreover, as Marion said: "We should be wetter than two mermaids by the time the boat touched the beach, and where would be the fun of stalking about the streets of Honolulu for a few hours in a dripping condition?"

It was with many a pang that we let the boat return without us, and sat on deck watching the increased loveliness of Oahu, as a golden glow touched the mountains, and the sea grew purple with reflected sunset clouds.

Before dark, Arthur came back, and brought with him one of the missionaries, who stayed to tea, and told us that unknown friends in Honolulu were disappointed in not welcoming us to their homes, for a visit of two young ladies from Massachusetts would have been an unusual pleasure to them. One gentleman had his carriage and horses waiting on the beach, meaning to give us a drive the moment we should land, so that we could have seen a good deal of town and country, even in two or three hours, but as we could not have arrived there with dry clothing his carriage cushions would have been ruined by salt water, and that thought tended to alleviate our feelings of regret for what we had lost. The missionary brought us some flowers — spider-lilies, he called them, with long, slender petals of purest white, and a strange, delicious odor. The land breezes that came to us had much of the same perfume, and the next day when I went on deck, soon after sunrise, a breath of sweet wind seemed to be following us from the depths of cool, rain-sprinkled forests.

I ventured to ask our guest if the only specimens of Sandwich Islanders we had seen might be taken as fair samples of the native population, and he replied with a smile that some of the boatmen were rather hard characters, and to judge of all their countrymen by a few of this class would lead us to doubt if missionary labors had improved them, outwardly, at least. Then he told us about the work of missions in this group of islands, and though we were familiar with the well-known fact that a more wonderful change has been wrought here within fifty years than can be accounted for merely by the labors of a little band of men and women, without a mighty power which we believe worked with them, I never quite realized before how great it was.

Before he left us, we gathered around the organ and sang the hymn,

> "Blest be the tie that binds
> Our hearts in Christian love."

and then, with messages from us to all the mission circle, whom we loved without seeing, he went away.

On deck, where the moonlight gave us a clear view of the peaceful town and its protecting mountains, I stood after he had bidden us farewell till the splash of his oars became inaudible, and tried to imagine Oahu as it was of old, the scenes of slaughter there, and fiery offerings to idol gods, but it was not easy to do so while I saw the moonbeams glistening on the roofs of Christian homes, and the white spire of a house of prayer plainly visible above the dark palms.

My musings were broken up by the noisy confusion preparatory to the heaving of the anchor; and the rattling of the chain, with a loud tramping of feet and calls to the men, sent me down into the cabin, after one farewell look of lingering regret at Honolulu.

Since that night we have had the true poetry of sailing. Day after day the Pacific is smooth as a lake, and from early morning until late in the evening we are on deck enjoying ourselves, and drawing comparisons between this ocean and the Atlantic that are unfavorable to the latter. I wonder if any one ever had four consecutive weeks of such weather as this on the ocean that washes our native shores. The afternoons are especially beautiful, for then we sail into a wide golden path of sunlight, and the sails keep off all glare from the deck, where we read aloud to each other, play chess, study, and write with no fear of the ink upsetting, and feast on oranges and bananas, mementoes of the Sandwich Islands, of which Arthur laid in a generous stock. It seems to us that we have never eaten real oranges before — the juice runs out of these in streams, and nearly half of it is lost, yet more remains than I ever saw in oranges purchased at home.

Who should appear the day after Mr. Curran left us but passenger number two, Marion's yellow cat, as gaunt as a famished wolf; but she did not appear to be very hungry, and after eating and drinking, she wandered around the ship in great uneasiness of body or mind, uttering mournful cries. It made Marion feel badly to see her Jim's favorite in such a state; and I was glad when the creature vanished again, for there was really something ghostly about her.

To-day we are becalmed. The sea is like pale blue satin, unbroken by the little waves that generally splash up out of the level surface as if excited by a sudden impulse of joy. The sun is scorching, and we are all so thirsty that frequent visits are made to the pantry for the purpose of concocting such mild beverages as water and citric acid, or lime-juice or syrups of various kinds,— all bad, to my taste, but an improvement on plain warm water flavored by the cask that has held it for a month. Compassion for the man at the wheel moved me this afternoon to offer him a glass of imitation lemonade, for he looked ready to melt under the hot sun, and while waiting for him to hand me back the glass, I saw two sharks following in our wake. I notified the second mate of their appearance. Harpoons were made ready, and hurled at the stealthily gliding monsters, missing their aim and only frightening them away, for which I was not sorry, as it takes them so long to die that my courage might have failed me at the sight of one of them squirming on deck, showing his cruel teeth.

Yesterday, we passed the Bashee Islands, and were impressed with the resemblance of one of them to a great stone image. It is a tall, narrow rock, standing quite alone, and the dark spots and crustations of shell near its summit led us to imagine a face. We called it an idol guarding the entrance to the China sea. As we sailed by it we bade farewell to the dear Pacific, where we had passed such happy days and felt we were drawing near to heathendom.

In the evening Mr Duncan asked us if we would like to go "for'ard" into the bows, and see the reflection of the moon on the sea ahead of the vessel. Marion, reposing on the skylight, with no better pillow for her head than a wooden box, said she was too happy to move, and Arthur was sleepy, but I went with Mr. Duncan past the forecastle and groups of respectful sailors, climbed the ladder to the "top-gallant-forecastle," and sat where I could see the spray flying up to wash the feet of the nymph with a lyre in her arms, — our figure-head — whose calm, white face looks steadily onward, with the same undaunted gaze, over wild billows or shining ripples. The golden track in which the ship had been sailing all the afternoon was changed to a sheet of pure silver, and my eyes followed it far away toward the great empire where a few more days' sailing will bring us. I seemed to be looking into the future, as I lost consciousness of myself and my companion in a reverie on what was before us,— experiences and acquaintances, perhaps, that will have a lasting influence upon my life and Marion's. Mr. Duncan's request that I would sing, brought me out of my dream, and he went to the cabin for my guitar. Marion came back with him, and assisted me in making melody that rang through the ship. Song after song was called for, when Arthur and Mr. Fordyce were added to our audience, and the proximity of the musical nymph must have inspired us, for you know our voices are not naturally powerful, and we sang that night as if possessed with the spirit of Euterpe. Our programme ended with Arthur's favorite "Gondolier," and I think the evening's entertainment was appreciated by all on board the "Lyra."

To-morrow we must begin to get ready for port, by packing sea-garments away, and bring out every thin dress we own, in preparation for intense heat, and if the present fair wind continues, the captain says we shall see China in two days.

CHAPTER V.

HONG KONG.

MARION'S STORY.

Hong Kong Harbor, May 18th.

I AM so full of longing to begin at once to tell you about this wonderful China, that going back a few days to connect this chronicle with what Amy last wrote requires some self-denial, though I am determined it shall not be my fault if you lose one of our experiences that may be of interest to you. Therefore you must know that last Thursday morning the row of islands between Hong Kong and the ocean came in sight, and our captain committed the daring act (as it seemed to us), of going through the Kap-Sing

Moon Pass, instead of entering the harbor by the Yat-Moon Pass, according to the general custom of navigators. These passes are rather narrow channels that separate the islands, and as the winds baffled his attempts to go through the Yat-Moon, Arthur announced his determination to try the other, although it has a dangerous name; a hidden rock lies in the middle of it, they say, and he went aloft with his glass to see if destruction was ahead, as the "Lyra" slowly sailed through Kap-Sing-Moon into safe waters.

I was not the only one on board who drew a long breath as we looked back and saw how narrow the channel was, and how easily a sudden gust of wind might have met and turned us back upon the rocks.

Soon two pilot-boats bore down upon us. They were Chinese sampans where families reside, knowing no other home than the little craft where they cook, eat, sleep, and worship their household gods as composedly as if four square feet of room for each person was an ample allotment. They were racing with each other, these two pilots, and the one who reached his goal first, climbed up to our deck like a squirrel, and made fast his floating habitation to the ship's stern, where two American girls leaned over with curious looks to gain their first idea of boat life in China. A woman sat near the rudder of the boat, and a baby hung at her back with a head that bobbed and rolled in a manner that threatened dislocation of the neck whenever his mother worked the scull oar, as she did from time to time, until her spouse had made a negotiation with Capt. Roslyn, and threw down a rope for her to attach to the sampan.

Early that morning my dear "Yaller" emerged from parts unknown after an absence of three or four weeks, more grievously afflicted than ever, it appeared, for incessant were her cries, and her exceeding leanness convinced us that she had not come from a region of plenty. Cousin Arthur, the most patient and forbearing of men, lost all patience with that unreasonable cat, and after mews in the saddest minor key had rung for hours in his ears, and he, with the rest of us, had wasted food and caresses upon the melancholy beast, his wrath broke forth:

"Girls! I don't know how long *you* can stand this sort of thing, but I am sure that Jim's cat and I have been shipmates long enough. Shall I give her to the pilot, Breezie?"

"Why, yes," I replied with a pang, at the idea of Jim's favorite becoming a stew, possibly, for a Chinese family. "If 'Yaller' refuses to stop this noise — which is chronic now, I'm afraid, she had better entertain those children in the sampan with it; but won't they eat her?"

"I pity them if they do," said the captain, emphatically. "Here, John! You wantchee cat?" (holding up my pet by the neck,)

John nodded, and pointed to his children as if to say that such a gift would be acceptable to them.

"Don't eat her, then," was the captain's warning, as he tied a rope to the cat and lowered her into the sampan, where two little boys and a girl held out their arms to receive their visitor. A grimace passed over the yellow visage of pilot John at the thought of the extremities to which his family must be reduced ere they should seek to appease the cravings of hunger by the bony frame of "Yaller," and he shook his head so vehemently that I was reassured. The cat settled herself on a coil of rope, as her young admirers surrounded her, and astonishment made her silent for a time. Such deeply seated grief as hers was not to be appeased by sudden change of circumstances, however, and late in the night I heard those piteous lamentations coming up from the darkness that enveloped the sampan.

The city lights were visible from our anchorage at one end of the harbor, where we stayed until daylight, then moved up among a fleet of vessels, and took a position directly opposite the city of Victoria.

Hong Kong Island consists of a chain of mountains. The highest of them, Victoria Peak, rises to an almost perpendicular height of eighteen hundred feet above the settlement which bears the same name, and the houses are built in regular terraces from the water's edge half way up the mountain, where they are scattered, and low-roofed bungalows nestle under the steep cliff.

This harbor seems entirely shut in by hills like a beautiful lake, for from our station we cannot see the pass by which we entered it, and I can hardly believe we 'are not landlocked by these curious hills. Those in the direction of the mainland abound in sand and decayed granite, and when the sunlight falls clearly upon them they have as many tints as a painter's palette. There are few trees to be seen anywhere, yet the mountains behind the city are saved from ruggedness by a soft, grassy covering, and they are deeply indented, as if a great hand had stroked them from their summits downward, leaving finger-marks.

On the sparkling green waters of the harbor are vessels of every size and nationality. Tall-masted clipper ships, English, French and German steamers, men-of-war, clumsy junks with bamboo sails, row-boats with passengers from some vessel to the city, or visitors from the city, several of whom favored the "Lyra" at an early hour after her anchor had been dropped. Amy and I agreed that there could not be a brighter, gayer scene than that of Hong Kong harbor on the morning of our arrival there, and in the bewilderment of having so many strange objects to look at we saw everything confusedly, as if Aladdin's lamp had suddenly raised up a vision of enchantment, of which every point must be taken in by eye and mind at once, before it should fade as suddenly as it appeared.

Several gentlemen came on board to pay their respects, and one of them brought us a kind of Chinese fruit, the lai-chee, which he tried to persuade me was eminently refreshing; but I, after taking one of them, (about the size of a horse chesnut), breaking off the thin reddish shell, and tasting it, was much inclined to throw it overboard. I have some lingering sense of propriety, however, if my friends do not credit me with it, and I stayed my hand.

"You don't like it!" said our visitor, in astonishment.

"I did n't say so."

"There was no need to say more than your face expressed," he said, laughingly. "In time you will prefer the lai-chee to one of your American pears."

"I can never compare it to anything but a very sweet onion," I answered, and Amy,

Hong Kong. 113

though always more courteous than I in making known her opinions, could not help showing that in this case they coincided with mine.

"To-morrow I will send you some mangos," said the gentleman, "and I want you each to eat a whole one before you condemn them, for these eastern fruits are unsurpassed by any in the world, and only require an educated taste to be highly appreciated."

"I am afraid to promise you that I will eat a whole one, if they are very large," said I, wishing our acquaintance would keep his foreign fruits for himself, if his taste is educated to appreciate them.

The appearance of Chinamen with large boxes saved me from making any more uncivil remarks. They opened them on the deck, and displayed sandal-wood fans, brooches and ear-rings of delicately carved ivory, rice-paper pictures, bamboo watch-chains, lacquered boxes, and a dozen other things.

"How can we speak to them?" I inquired of Mr. Day, the gentleman who bestowed the lai-chees upon us.

"You must talk pidgin-English, or in other words talk as silly nurse-maids do to little children; put an "ee" on the end of half your words, and leave out all your articles and prepositions. I will trade for you, and show you how to beat down a Chinaman. It is quite an art."

"Please ask him, then, how much that little carved box is worth."

"How muchee pricee?" demanded our interpreter, pointing to it.

"One dollar quart" ($1.25).

"One dollar quart! No can do, John. That b'long too muchee pricee. My give you fifty cents."

"How can you" — (have the impudence to beat him down to less than half of what he asks, was the unspoken part of my sentence, and as usual it was written on my face.)

"Oh! you must learn to beat down these traders. A Chinaman always asks at least half as much again as he knows an article is worth, and does not expect to get his price unless he has a green customer. He really would not respect you if you gave him what he demanded at first, "*Fifty cents*," he repeated with emphasis."

"One dollar," said the Chinaman, coming down a little. "Fifty cents!" "Seventy-five cents?" said the trader pathetically, but a stern repetition of "Fifty cents," reduced him to submission. "All light! You takee," was his concession, and I felt as if I had robbed him when he handed the box to Mr. Day, who put it in my hand.

"You need not be troubled," he said. No Chinaman would ever lose by a bargain of this kind, and as he lets you have it for fifty cents, you may be sure he makes a profit on it.

"I don't see how I can ever bring myself

to 'grind the faces' of the heathen in that manner," was my rejoinder.

"You will be cheated out of a great deal of cash if you do not," said Mr. Day, evidently considering me the most obstinate and intractable of young women.

The captain and mates joined the group around the box of "curios," (everything that a foreigner in China would be likely to buy for presentation to friends at home is called "curio"), and Mr. Fordyce, with his usual recklessness, seemed inclined to buy half the man's stock, and to lavish it upon Amy and me, reserving some trinkets to take home to his sisters; but with the sternness of a judicious parent I bade him save his money for sensible purchases, and refused to accept anything but a tiny charm for my watch-chain.

The noontide heat made us realize that we were indeed in China, and sent Amy down into the cool cabin, while I stayed on deck to enjoy it. The great wall of mountains seemed to reflect the absorbed heat of months upon the harbor; and Victoria Peak, where the grass grows scantily near its summit, and a ledge of rock shines with moisture from some little rill, resembled a giant with perspiring forehead.

All sorts of characters came on board that day; shoemakers, tailors, washerwomen, merchants or clerks from the great business houses; captains from neighboring vessels, and we had no chance to go ashore, even if we had been allowed to do so. "You shall see enough of Hong Kong," our captain promised us, "but I do not want you to go about in the city before you are somewhat accustomed to Asiatic heat which, even here, with the harbor breeze, makes Amy look like a wilted white petunia. To-morrow you shall ride to church in a sedan-chair." With this novel prospect we retired on that Saturday night when our last caller had departed. He was a middle-aged captain, and discoursed to

Arthur of jib-booms and studding-sails, while I lost consciousness of him in a bamboo reclining chair, and mortified my cousins by two startling snores.

Sunday morning was bright and hot, and every vessel had on its gayest attire of flags. A Bethel flag floated from the "Lyra's" mast-head as a notice to our neighbors that religious services were to be held on board, and the captain and second mate of the barque "Hazelton" were added to our usual audience. At ten, we girls with Arthur and Mr. Fordyce were rowed ashore to attend church. On one of the many stone landings that are built upon the Praya (a wide street, by the waterside), we encountered a crowd of coolies with bare legs and great hats, and their sedan-chairs ready to receive us. Imagine a cane seat in a box, shaded by a canopy; two long poles, of which the ends rest upon the shoulders of Chinamen (after the occupant has walked into it backward, as a horse goes into the carriage-shafts), and you know what a sedan-chair is; but the delights of riding in one can never be approached by the imagination. Two pidgin English commands must be employed for this mode of travel. If your bearers are pattering along at too lively a pace, you call "Man-man!" and they slacken their speed; if you want them to go faster, you say "Chop-chop!" If your desire is to stop, you pound on the side of the chair that is nearest the place where they shall halt, and repeat "Man-man" in a tone of decision.

We wended our way up, up, up, to Dr. Leggs's beautiful chapel on one of the higher terraces, passing through narrow streets, where the noise of business went on as though there were no such day as Sunday, and when seated in the marble-paved building, through whose stone arches the song of birds and the rustle of leaves stole in, a quiet accompaniment to the minister's voice, I heard also a far-off hum of heathen life from the toiling world below.

"God is our refuge and strength, a very present help in trouble. Therefore will not we fear though the earth be removed, and though the mountains be carried into the midst of the sea." That psalm was read from the pulpit, and never before had the words impressed me with such solemnity, and at the same time as such a cause for rejoicing.

After church we found our coolies in attendance with the chairs, and they carried us down from the peaceful chapel under the mountain's shadow to the boat landing, whence our "Skimmer," propelled by its crew of boys, shot over the half mile of water to the "Lyra's" anchorage.

In the afternoon Arthur invited me to attend the Chinese service with him in the same church, Union Chapel, it is called, and we made the voyage to the city in a sampan for the sake of novelty. Arthur hailed one that was floating near us, and asked the

Hong Kong Woman. — Page 120.

proprietor how many he had on board,—meaning the number of oarsmen.

"Seven piecee man," was the prompt rejoinder, and we thought that so many pairs of arms would take us ashore in good time, but found when we were seated in the cabin (a square hole in the deck sheltered by a bamboo awning) that "seven piecee man" included the mother of the family, with her infant slung around her neck, a girl of about eighteen years, and two small boys, beside the man himself and his elder sons. Our progress was not rapid, and when a heavy yellow sail was hoisted, the sampan lay over so far that I kept sliding off my seat, and the water splashed up on the deck. Novelty atones for many inconveniences, sometimes, and I was interested in watching the Chinese family, especially the girl, who sat near me, rowing with bare, muscular arms that looked as if their owner was used to doing the work of at least "*one* piecee man." She was so miserable and neglected, this poor girl, with her soiled, ragged dress, rough, uncovered head, and a face expressive of nothing but a heavy discontent, that I longed to say a kind word to her, but of course I could not, and I tried to show my interest in her by a friendly smile when she looked at me. She observed me with astonishment, and her hard face softened a little as she moved her oar with renewed vigor.

Ten cents for each passenger is the usual sampan fare, and Arthur gave the man twenty-five cents when we landed, yet his avaricious soul was not satisfied, and he loudly clamored for more, no doubt thinking that we, having lately arrived at Hong Kong, might be easily cheated. We left him grumbling on the wharf, and, waving off numerous chair-coolies, who were importunate as hackmen in a depot, bent our steps towards the chapel.

There are so many things to observe during

our walk that I hardly realized how very hot I was. Groups of men sat in shady places on the street corners, playing some kind of game with small stones or coins. From their deep absorption in it we judged them to be gambling.

Little girls played about with heavy babies fastened on their backs, and my wonder was aroused by the proper behavior of these Chinese infants, who never seemed to mind if their heads did swing like pendulums during the progress of their sisters' pastime, but blinked their narrow black eyes in resignation to the ills of life, as if sustained under them by the wisdom of Confucius. I didn't pity them, after all, but my heart and back ached in sympathy with the poor little maidens, who, at the age of eight, begin to learn a Chinese woman's hard lot of servitude, and have to carry burdens even at their play.

Women stood in the door-ways enjoying

their afternoon gossip but no white ladies were taking their walks abroad, and the stares I encountered led us to conclude that it is not the custom here for them to do so.

About fifty Chinese were assembled in the cool, quiet chapel to hear a sermon in their own language, which failed to edify me, though it gave me pleasure to observe their faces while they listened to better things than the crowds below have knowledge of; and the earnest, intelligent look of many made me sure that the truth was making light within them;—only a glimmering light in some hearts, perhaps, yet even a spark makes a great change where utter darkness once reigned. "Rock of Ages" was sung in closing the services, and I could not help joining in softly with our English words, knowing their meaning to be the same as that expressed in the strange tongue of my Chinese brothers and sisters.

As they passed out, kindly greetings seemed to be exchanged, and I noticed one woman tenderly helping another, whose tiny, pinched feet, made walking down the steep hill both dangerous and painful to her. A "little flock," truly, were these compared with the thousands of idolaters in the city; nevertheless to them belongs the promise of "the kingdom."

On Monday morning a basket of mangos came with Mr. Day's compliments. They are large, oval fruit, with bright yellow skins, flat stones, and a peculiar flavor, reminding me so much of a paint-shop that I was glad I had not promised to eat a whole one. Amy took a fancy to them, and not discerning any flavor of turpentine, accused me of having too much imagination, but I have heard the same idea expressed by other people who are not fond of them.

Traders flocked on board all the morning, and we should have been well cheated if Mr.

Duncan had not come to the rescue, preventing us from buying ornaments of common bone, which we had been earnestly assured were made of the finest ivory, and putting us on our guard against the wily arts of the heathen.

After dinner callers came, and I was pleasantly engaged in conversation with one of them, a native of the "Hub," when a flash of brass buttons suddenly illumined our cabin, as three officers from the man-of-war "Ariadne" walked in. One of them was dark, slender, romantic-looking, like the heroes of a certain class of novels, whose aim in life is to elope with blondes, and run their swords through the bodies of their rivals. (My simile is drawn from unprofitable perusals of very light literature in the days of early youth). One had a pleasant, boyish face, and the third was stout, good-natured, and not far from the meridian of life. They gave us a cordial welcome to the harbor of Hong Kong, and declared themselves refreshed by the sight of two new young ladies, as for months their vessel had been lying in these waters, and every spectacle that the city affords had lost its novelty to them long ago, they said; and when Amy told them that neither her cousin nor herself had ever set foot on the deck of a man-of-war, delight was expressed in their countenances. I am sure they thought that rare entertainment was provided for them in the chance of showing off the naval department to the uninitiated. They were certainly in a condition to be "tickled by a straw," if *we* could thus be the humble means of raising their spirits, and glad to be useful in the world, even to navy officers, we received with friendliness, their promises to be very neighborly, and accepted, with our captain's approval, their offer to come on the following afternoon, and take us on board the "Ariadne" in style.

When callers had left us to our own devices,

we went ashore to see the city more satisfactorily than the sedan rides to church had shown it to us on Sunday. The usual "scrimmage" with chair coolies was undergone upon the landing steps, and as it was impossible for each of us to occupy more than one chair, only six Chinamen were made happy, and many discomfited, as we proceeded along the Praya into a square where stands the City Hall, a handsome edifice, and near it is a space enclosed for a cricket ground; then past the barracks, up a shady, hilly road to the mountains. We saw a brook running along at the base of one of them, where much of the city laundry-work is done, and the hill-side was white with the clothes laid out to dry there.

Going through a great gate, and leaving our conveyances outside, we mounted wide stone steps, and found ourselves in the Public Garden, where on Thursday afternoons the English band plays, and the residents of

Hong Kong promenade. There I got into one of my ecstasies over the harbor view which lay below us, and sat down to indulge in it, but I was hurried off to my chair to be borne higher yet, through roads that twist and turn about under those towering green heights. The houses of the aristocracy are there; cool stone buildings, in the arches of whose wide verandahs birds twitter, and plants wave their great leaves, and one looks out over bamboos that half hide the city roofs, sees the fleet in the harbor, and the far-away hills of China, and thinks how very good ought to be the people who live amid such loveliness. Thus it was with me yesterday when we took tiffin (lunch) at one of these houses. The hostess was an English lady, kindly disposed toward the brown-faced sailor-girls, but exceedingly quiet and reserved, and I felt as if I were walking about in an immense Chinese workbox (the house smelt like one), and was not at my ease all the afternoon. Polished floors, tall vases, lacquer work were everywhere, a punkah fanned us at table, butter was passed in a bottle and taken out with a spoon; Chinamen, clad in pure white, served us noiselessly, rice and curried chicken were the chief substantials, and lai-chees the ornamentals; and I, common-place Marion Gilmer from Boston, felt in a vague way out of place among such foreign surroundings; feared to open my lips, lest some sea phrase or Yankee inaccuracy of speech should grate upon the ears of the English lady, and yearned for the "Lyra's" cabin and solid dinner of "lobscouse" and beans.

Amy enjoyed everything (except the melted butter), and fitted in with her surroundings in a ladylike manner. The elegancies of life never fluster her, and they couldn't do it if she should return to them after years of uncivilized life on prairies or ocean.

On the afternoon appointed for our visit

to the "Ariadne," a large, cushioned boat, manned by ten oarsmen, was in attendance at the gangway, and accompanied, of course, by Arthur, we went to fulfil our engagement with the officers. The novel hero, Lieut. Neufville, came for us, and the others received us on board the man-of-war, which is not an imposing vessel, but all her appointments were new to us and very interesting.

The men went through some of their exercises at the guns, and after watching them, and walking up and down the beautifully clean decks, we were taken down into the dark mess-room where the sailors live, and through the engine-room, bringing up finally at the ward-room, and there we sat down to be entertained by the officers with things belonging especially to their own domain. Albums and large collections of foreign views were looked over, but they were nothing at all in comparison with a sketch-book of Lieut. Neufville's, which displayed an artistic and sarcastic talent truly remarkable. One could have wished the sarcasm to have been omitted in some instances, as in a picture of a pretty girl riding in a sedan-chair, which was entitled "The Young Missionary and the Benighted Heathen." Now I could see no reason why those who come out to China to do the heathen good should not have their strength saved by occasional rides, and the honest calling of the chair-coolie is rendered no more degrading by the carrying of missionaries than of officers or merchants; but that picture implied on the part of the sketcher a hint of inconsistency on the part of missionaries, and it called forth a remark from me which led us into a deep argument on the responsibility of the heathen, and whether the work of missions is entirely useless and unprofitable. I need not tell you that this position was not mine. To the best of my ability I withstood it; but in truth, dear friend, I never thought much about the heathen till I came here, and although not believing one of my opponent's words, I could not answer them with the wisdom of one who had considered the matter, and I was growing hotter in that ward-room than a burning sun could have made me, both from indignation at the lieutenant's sophistries, and my own inability to say the right thing, when relief came in the form of ice-cream. While we partook of that luxury, a waiter-boy stood behind my chair and helped on the cooling process with a large palm-leaf fan, and my equanimity was restored in-less than fifteen minutes, yet I could not dismiss the grave subject from my mind. As we were rowed back to the "Lyra" I told myself that to gain a clear understanding of what the Bible reveals to us with regard to our duties towards God and man, is more important than to learn to follow the windings of a skeptical reasoning which has no more substance than a puff of smoke, when one tries to grasp and hold it.

The question uppermost with us at present concerns a visit to Canton. We certainly *must* see a purely Chinese city before we sail for the Phillipine Islands; and Hong Kong, where the English element is strong, will not give us all the ideas of the Chinese Empire we wish to gain.

A kind letter came recently from one of the Canton missionaries, Mr. Worthington, who had heard of us through friends of his in New York whom we know well, and he invites us to visit him; so it is decided that a week must be devoted to Canton, and we shall go there in a day or two. Arthur does not care to leave the ship for a whole week, but he will send Mr. Duncan with us, and come himself a few days later.

This letter is finished just in time for the Pacific Mail steamer, which comes in about the fourth of every month, and leaves near the twelfth. The "America" was the one that came in this month, and we went on board of her to take breakfast. Such a steamer I never saw before, or even thought of seeing! A grand hotel floating on the water, she might almost be compared to, and it made my patriotism rise to a high degree when I watched her steaming through Ly-Moon Pass. She brought us a dear, long letter from you, which we have not finished reading yet, though every word of it will soon be as familiar as "The House that Jack Built." Arthur calls for selections from it when he wants to be entertained, and then laughs as much as if he understood every one of the standard jokes that are only appreciated by a school-girl's intellect.

Farewell till next mail. But it will be Amy's turn to write, then, won't it? and I shall have other letters to send, so I may write next from Manila, or Iloilo, or whatever outlandish place the "Lyra" is ordered to, and until then, farewell.

MARION.

CHAPTER VI.

TRIP TO CANTON.

Hong Kong Harbor, June 4th.

A WEEK in Canton has given me materials for a volume, which, even if not of much interest to the public, would be perused without weariness, I believe, by the partial eye of friendship. I will content myself with something short of a volume, however, and try to write this letter to you, my dear girl, within the proper limits.

You must follow in spirit your two friends, as with Mr. Duncan, on the morning of May twenty-fifth, they were quietly steaming up the Canton river in a drizzling rain. From the

Scenery and mode of travel in China. — Page 141.

windows of the pilot-house we looked out upon the yellow stream, the fresh green of rice-fields along the banks, the darker, shining foliage of the trees, and a tall pagoda rising up here and there. We passed the village of Whampoa, whose neighboring hills are covered with rows of Chinese tombs, and in the middle of the afternoon arrived at Canton, where we saw the heathen world in full force on the landing, and crowds of boats.

Mr. Worthington met us, and took us in a sampan to his house, a dreary, blackish edifice on the edge of the canal. Passing through a ground-floor that was very cellar-like, we ascended a flight of stairs into cheerful rooms, and there stood the missionary family with warm greetings for the visitors from their own far-off land.

Mr. Worthington is a scholarly-looking man, whose careworn face shows the traces of many toiling years, and is rather stern in its gravity; but when one of his little daughters clasps his hand with a loving, upward glance, or when he turns to one of us to say some kind word, a beaming smile irradiates every feature. His wife is just what one would suppose a missionary's wife ought to be,—a true lady with genial tact and quiet self-possession; and the children, though perfectly unaffected in their manners, had such a way of assuming their responsibility in our entertainment as family guests, that I regarded them with pleased surprise, and decided that there must be something in the influence around the children of missionaries that gives them a thoughtfulness and maturity beyond their years.

But the eldest daughter! How can I describe her? Faith Worthington is much younger than I am, a year or two younger than Marion, and no more like any other girl of seventeen whom I have known than a broad, deep river is like a noisy, shallow brook. There seems to be an unfathomable depth in Faith—in those blue eyes of hers, in the calm, fair face that to me ever expresses one Bible verse: "Thou wilt keep him in perfect peace whose mind is stayed on Thee." That peace is unruffled by weariness or the din of heathendom outside the windows.

"How can you study Chinese with such a noise always in your ears?" I asked, and they acknowledged the difficulty.

"But," said little Agnes, "you know it is never going to stop, except at night, and the studying must be done, for though we have talked Chinese from our cradles, we have to work hard to learn the written language." I could not doubt it, recalling the mysterious characters on tea-chests and packages of fire-crackers.

In the evening the weekly missionary prayer-meeting was held at Mr. Worthington's, and about ten ladies and gentlemen came in with as little formality as if they were members of one family. They are, in fact, united by a tie even stronger than that of kindred,— the same deep interest in their Master's work which has led them to give up houses, and brethren, and lands for His sake and the gospel's. We were welcomed by them most warmly, as if they considered us representatives of the Christian friends whose prayers in behalf of foreign missions ascend from the churches of America.

I have been to some missionary prayer-meetings at home that were rather dull, it must be confessed. The pastor would call on "Brother G." to "give us some information with regard to the Mahratta mission," but the brother had not received his *Missionary Herald* in time to prepare for the meeting, and there was a general lack of information that was depressing. In the prayers for the conversion of the heathen there was not always apparent an intense realization of their need, and I recalled those by-gone Sunday evenings, as we knelt with that devoted little company of laborers, and heard the earnest outpouring of their requests as those who felt their feebleness, yet were strong in the promise "Lo I am with you alway." So much was expressed of the comfort they felt in knowing that many in America were praying for them, that I said to myself, "When I go home I will tell every one I know to pray more for missionaries than they ever did before."

The return of daylight was a relief after a night disturbed by heat, mosquitos, the cries of watchmen who walk the streets,— making at intervals a fearful din (to warn evil-doers of their approach, and kindly allow them time for escape), and the squeals of quadrupeds in the next building, a pig-market.

I went into the verandah to watch Canton life swarming on the sidewalk which separates the house from the muddy canal, and found yet greater interest in the sampans wedged side by side in a long row. There, children frolic and are disciplined by the parental hand. Wooden bottles hang at the waists of some of them to increase their chances of escape from drowning when they tumble overboard.

"There must be a wedding in the sampan that lies nearest the landing steps," said Agnes.

"What makes you think so?"

"There seems to be something going on there, and I heard a girl's voice wailing for a long time in the night. That is what they always do on the night before they are married."

"Because they are going to have such a hard time," added Mattie, the youngest Worthington.

"Do they have a wedding ceremony?"

"These boat people do not go through so many forms as those of a higher class," Faith told us. "For three days their friends visit them, and a pig is generally roasted (that means about the same as wedding cake), and at some time during the three days the young couple do obeisance before the ancestral tablets; but first the bride leaves her father's boat and goes to a new home, to scrub and row harder than ever in her girlhood. Do you wish to pay this bride a visit?"

"Will she like it?"

"Oh yes! it will be considered an honor," said Mrs. Worthington, and six of us went down to the canal, leaving Mr. Duncan to survey the scene from the verandah, as Marion vetoed his accompanying us for the reason that he would take up more room than three people of moderate size, and might upset the bridal sampan. I wonder now that we all could have packed ourselves into that little boat, but we did, and sat in Turkish attitudes to take up less space, while the bride, clad in flaming red, with chenille flowers towering above her shining black hair, came forward at her mother-in-law's bidding and saluted us with reverential courtesies, then handed a tray of refreshments — little squares of cake, and tea without milk or sugar, in what looked like doll's cups. The cake was abominable in the extreme, and I ate it with a spirit of politeness at a great personal sacrifice, and partook of the tea. Mrs. Worthington suggested afterwards that it was probably made with the muddy canal water, and I was grateful to her for not putting the idea into my head before. All the politeness requisite to such an occasion we left to the ladies and children who spoke Chinese, and contented ourselves with smiling graciously at the bride and her mother.

A group of men collected on the sidewalk to see us go up the landing steps and enter the house, and a general excitement seemed to prevail in the vicinity of the sampan which had been so honored.

An English clergyman, Archdeacon Gray, called to see us, and kindly offered his services

Trip to Canton. 149

as a guide about the city, for he is well known and popular among the Chinese, and has access to some places that few foreigners are privileged to enter.

We set out in chairs that afternoon, Mr. Duncan, Marion, and I, our reverend guide leading the procession through the narrow streets, most of them about six feet in width, and full of people. Our first halt was at the house of one of the Chinese aristocracy, whose owner had given the Archdeacon permission to show strangers over his mansion during his absence at the Imperial Court. There were lofty halls ornamented with gilding and carving, the greenness of conservatories appeared through high latticed windows. After walking through many rooms, we came to a court, on the other side of which were the lady's apartments, and a group of female slaves stood there, smiling and staring at us. Mr. Gray told us to go into the boudoir while he waited with Mr. Duncan on the other side of the court. After a little hesitation at what seemed like the coolest kind of impudence, and passing the great lady herself we surveyed her rooms, while she surveyed us with timid interest, and did not look at all affronted by our bold proceedings.

The next stopping-place was at an "opium divan," a dark room like a tomb, furnished with settees, where were extended several poor wretches in different stages of stupefaction.

There were so many things to arrest our attention that we did not resume our chairs at once, but walked along the dark alleys with about thirty Chinese at our heels, who stopped whenever we did, and stared at us without ceremony, yet not rudely. A china-shop was visited, and wonders in the way of painted vases and dishes were shown us; then we looked in at a flour-mill, where the grinding was performed in the most primitive manner by buffaloes walking in a circle and causing one great stone to revolve upon another.

"Do you see that sign?" asked the Archdeacon, stopping before what appeared to be a butcher's shop, and pointing to a gilt lettered board. "I will translate it for you— 'Black cats always for sale here.' Over this stall is a cat and dog refreshment saloon. Will you come up, young ladies?"

We turned our astonished gaze from the counter on which a man was chopping up a dog's tail in delicate slices, as if it were a Bologna sausage, and went up-stairs to see people eating hot stews that had a peculiar, though not unsavory smell.

"What are you eating?" inquired the Archdeacon, taking up one man's saucer. "Black cat," was the answer translated to us. Another man, on being similarly questioned, replied, "Dog," with a grin implying that he knew such fare was not common, even among his countrymen, in polite circles.

"I wished you to be able to tell your friends in America that you have actually witnessed this thing," said the Archdeacon as we gladly followed him down the winding stairs.

Then began a tour among the temples. First to the Temple of Letters, where the effigies of the authors of letters and of the printing art are enthroned in state; next, to the Temple of the Five Hundred Genii, a great building, where one wanders through a labyrinth of galleries, courts, and rooms. We sat in the visitors' hall, and were served with clear tea and dried fruit, while the rain poured down into a courtyard upon which the hall opened, washing the leaves of tropical plants growing there. After a little rest, one of the monks showed us the five hundred wooden figures who sit in a ghostly row around a large, dark room. They are the images of those who were devoted to the service of Buddha while on earth, and in a

Image of Buddha. — Page 152.

Trip to Canton. 155

great case was the gilded figure of the god himself.

As I stood in that gloomy room, and heard deep tones of thunder echoing through the building, it seemed to me like the voice of God expressing His displeasure at all idol worship, and I thanked Him there with all my heart that He had led me to know Him, the only true God, as a Father and a Saviour.

In another room was a tall pagoda looming up through the darkness, with an image of some deity sitting in every story. It rained so heavily that we waited in one of the courts, where the monks treated us with great politeness, and gave us more tea, a refreshment that I, for one, could have dispensed with, my throat and tongue having been well scalded before, for hot tea, minus milk, to one unused to it, is very fiery in its effects. Our little parasols caused much amusement to the monks, who, on being allowed to examine them, burst into peals of wondering laughter. One of them pointed to Mr. Gray's umbrella, and said, "*That* I can understand, but is this really an umbrella?"

"It is of no use to wait for the rain to cease," said the Archdeacon finally, and we took our chairs again and went on to the Temple of Longevity. There we were received by another party of monks in a room of which one whole side opened on a pond, surrounded by green bushes, and nearly covered with floating lotus leaves. More tea was given us (hotter, if possible, than that partaken of in the other temples), also preserved lai-chees and ginger. A venerable monk was seized with curiosity concerning Marion's dress, a white picqué, and stole quietly up to lay an examining finger upon it, but meeting an expression of reproval in the Archdeacon's face, he drew back, and contented himself with asking some questions about us, which met with a grave response. We then visited the God of Longevity in another room, and returned to Mr. Worthington's through gathering darkness and descending showers.

Pagoda. — Page 156.

Once, when the rest of our party, preceding me, had disappeared around a corner, a feeling of loneliness took strong hold of me, and a fear that I might be carried off by my coolies; but it was suddenly put to flight by a remembrance of the psalm that describes the idols of the heathen, "the work of men's hands," and then exhorts Israel to "trust in the Lord." Peace came to me in the gloomy street as I went on, thinking "I will fear no evil, for Thou art with me," and soon we reached the hospitable dwelling by the canal, where Faith was watching for us at the door.

For the next day, a visit at another missionary home was planned, and we walked through the city to a pleasant house near the river, where we dined, after visiting the mission hospital across the way. The wife of the physician who has the charge of it showed us over the building, and took us into a neat little chapel, where those needing medical advice, while waiting for Dr. Kerr to attend to their poor ailing bodies, are induced to listen to a native teacher, as he leads them to consider their souls' health.

Our kind conductor of the previous afternoon had promised to call at four o'clock to show us a few more temples, and after a very social dinner, we went out into the heat and glare to increase our stock of Chinese information. One place we were warned against by some of our lady friends. "Don't go into the 'Chamber of Horrors' if you can help it," they said, and the caution only made Marion determined to see a place whose title and associations were so grim. I have not a taste for horrors myself, but thought we might safely trust the Archdeacon to show us no unprofitable sights, and forgot all about the the matter in a visit to the Examination Hall.

Passing through a building that was much like a temple, we found beyond it a grassy court with long rows of what look like horse-sheds, but they are really cells for 17,000 men who come here every three years to be examined for the degrees of A.M. and B.A. Subjects for essays are appointed by judges, and each competitor is shut up in a cell with pen and paper to try for an honor whose glory will be reflected upon his posterity, if he succeeds in gaining it. Sometimes a man is found dead in his cell from the effects of a long mental strain.

It was a very quiet place that afternoon, and I wandered over the soft green sward, and in and out of the cells, looking up at the floating clouds, and dreamily imagining the eager ambition, the bitter disappointment in the hearts of thousands who in past years came to this arena for mental combat; thinking of the exultant pride with which many had departed, bearing the coveted honor, the reward of their toil, and then had left it inscribed on marble tablets, for their sons to glory in, while in spiritual darkness their souls passed away from earthly scenes. Ah, how hard we work in this world to gain a little, and how soon we have to give it up when gained! The Chinese, whose ambition leads them here, know nothing of "a better and an enduring substance," but in lands where people do know of it, many spend their lives in ignoring that knowledge and striving painfully after what they must lose. That seems the saddest thing.

Thus musing, I strolled on, almost forgetting the rest of my party, and came face to face with a being so hideous that I started back, half believing it to be the embodied spirit of the hatred and despair that reign in this place every three years; but it was only an old woman who wanted "cash," the smallest of coins, and held out her skinny hand with a leer that fairly made me cold.

"Miss Amy!" called Mr. Duncan, and came to find me. "Has this old lady fastened you here by a spell?"

"Something like it," said I, with a sudden sense of relief, and walking back to the "Judges' Hall" with him. "Did you ever see such faces as these old Chinese women have? Yet many of the young ones are really pleasing."

"These poor souls have had nothing in their

lives to look back upon with any solid satisfaction, and have nothing to look forward to, according to their priests, but life hereafter in the shape of animals," said my companion, "and a miserable old age shows itself in their faces."

" Do they believe that?" I asked.

" Yes, Mr. Worthington told me that when a a woman dies they suppose her soul will pass into the body of some animal, and after many changes, as from the meanest animal to the noblest, she will at length become a man."

" *Then* she can really enjoy some privileges," said I, rather amused, yet sad at the thought of my poor Chinese sisters and their degradation.

" Everything is turned upside down on this side of the world," said Mr. Duncan. " In America, if we believed in the transmigration of souls, we should say that the men must pass through many changes and much discipline before they could be worthy to become women."

" Do you mean that for a sarcasm on the Woman's Rights question?" I inquired, inwardly reproving myself for imputing sarcasm to one in whose composition there is no shade of it.

"I only meant to express my honest opinion that your sex is ahead of mine in most of the virtues," replied "our mate," in a tone that conveyed some reproach to me for misunderstanding him, and then we all resumed our chairs, leaving Examination Hall and its spectral women behind us.

Next upon the Archdeacon's programme came a great temple consecrated to the God of Walled Cities, and there for the first time we saw idol worship, as we passed a kneeling figure, and heard him muttering his supplications to an ugly image. The Archdeacon had the great privilege of taking us up into the god's bedroom, a place so sacred that few Chinese, even, are permitted to enter it, except on special occasions; and there were beds, washstands, shoes, and clothes for the colossal images, the God of Walled Cities and wife, who sit there grimly regarding the intruders upon their seclusion. Many a new dress or pair of shoes, does the goddess receive from ladies whose prayers are supposed to have been graciously answered by her.

Coming out of this temple we saw the "Chamber of Horrors," a court with ten cells in it, and in each cell were represented by little wooden figures the tortures to be expected by wicked people in the next world; some being smothered, some boiled or ground in pieces, and finally at the tenth world appearing in the form of wild animals. In every cell were the spirits of good men (all wooden) serenely regarding these tortures from an elevated position upon what are called "Heights of the Blessed." Thus even the heathen seem to know there is a difference between right and wrong. I wonder if that is what Paul meant when he spoke of "their consciences meanwhile accusing or else excusing one another."

Marion was disappointed in the Chamber of Horrors, and finding more comedy than tragedy in the aspect of the wooden sufferers, felt herself aggrieved by those ladies who had so greatly raised her expectations.

The Temple of the God of War was the grandest one we visited. Stately trees shaded its courtyard, and the slanting rays of the sun flickered through their leaves upon strange and ancient architecture.

"This is the Street of the Dead," said the Archdeacon, as we wended our way through a street where stores on either hand were stocked with fans, shoes, pipes — all sorts of wares generally desired by the living.

" All these things are bought for the dead, and are put into their coffins, or in the tombs, under the supposition that the spirit, wherever he may be, will take pleasure in using them," explained our reverend friend. He then took us up a lofty flight of steps leading directly from the street to the clock-tower, where we saw a real water-clock. You will understand by the name that the time is indicated in some way by the dropping of water, and that is all I know about it, for I was then too tired to listen to any explanations, and wearily leaned over the parapet of the tower to look down upon the great city spread out beneath us, growing more weary at the thought of all the toil going on there.

"Oh, another temple!" I sighed to Marion, as Archdeacon Gray told Mr. Duncan that we must not fail to see the Temple of the Five Genii, who, as the tradition goes, once came to this city seated on five rams, and brought prosperity.. They were called Fire, Earth, Water, Wood and Metal, and are represented by five tablets. We saw the original rams — five blocks of stone, each bearing some resemblance to a ram's head.

Behind this temple is a massive tower, six hundred years old, where hangs a huge bell covered with Chinese characters. The people think that if this bell is ever struck misfortune will come to Canton. Then we saw a small temple dedicated to virtuous women; then the Temple of Confucius, and finally a Mohammedan mosque.

At last, I am happy to say, we returned to the house where we had dined, feeling very grateful for having seen what must be remembered all our lives with interest.

A cup of delicious tea (with as much milk and sugar as I wanted) revived me so far that I could join in pleasant games and conversation, and walk home with Faith and Mr. Worthington; but all night I was in a queer state, fancying myself exploring peculiarities of Chinese life against my will, surrounded by a gang of noisy heathen, and vainly wishing I could rest my tired feet and brain.

Image of Confucius. — Page 168.

CHAPTER VII.

CANTON.

"I WANT to give you a peep into the life of Chinese aristocracy," said Faith to us the next morning as she came into the verandah, where stood Marion and myself, absorbed as usual in the moving panorama below, and laid her hands lovingly on our shoulders. "Does my brown apron astonish you? I have been filling the lamps (my hands are clean now), for I can't trust the servants with the lamp oil, they will persist in using it to cook their own food with,— such is their inconvenient taste."

"Where are you going to take the young ladies, Faith?" asked Mrs. Worthington.

"To call on the Minquas if they would like to go, mamma. You know one of the Minqua girls is a Christian, a member of our church, and she asked me two weeks ago to come and see her. To visit the family of a Canton merchant will be a chance that few foreign ladies have," added Faith, turning to us.

We assured her of the pleasure we should feel in availing ourselves of that chance, and in the afternoon set out with Faith and Agnes for the abode of the Minquas, attended through the streets by a frightful old Chinaman, "the husband of our amah" (nurse), Aggie told us. A porter threw open the great iron gate, and we entered the inevitable sky-roofed, stone-paved court, where we were met by two young ladies, who took our hands and murmured "How you do?" in a shy, pretty way, then led us into their sitting-room, and gave us some very hard seats of black, polished wood. There were a good many women in the room; some were Minqua's daughters, or daughters-in-law, and some attendants, and they were all thrown into a state of agreeable excitement by our visit; but beyond "How you do?" the knowledge of English did not extend in the family, and few of them had attained even to that. Faith and Agnes talked enough for us all, however, and the ladies treated us with the gentlest courtesy, offering tea, dried fruit, and cake whose flavor made me wonder if the higher classes, as well as Faith's domestics, used lamp oil in the culinary department. It was peanut oil, we were told afterwards, and that is used for lamps as well as for cooking. Wishing to make up for conversational deficiencies, they sent a servant for their robes of state and exhibited them to us, then intimated by gestures that they would like to have us try them on. Faith laughingly acquiesced, and so we did also, standing meekly while they arrayed us in garments that glittered with gold and silver embroidery. I got a glimpse of myself in a mirror, and started at my resemblance to the little women you see on Chinese fans. Great was the excitement produced as they caused us to promenade in the court, and all the ladies, as well as the female slaves and two brothers who had joined the party, laughed and clapped their hands like children. Poor Marion, overcome by the weight of her finery and the intense heat of the afternoon, leaned against a railing and seemed ready to sink, seeing which, the head of the house of Minqua, a pleasant looking young man, fanned her assiduously with a huge palm-leaf. We were soon divested of our uncomfortable splendor and given more tea. I was also offered a pipe to smoke, which I declined. I must not omit one part of our entertainment, the exhibition of our hostesses' small feet; about three inches they average (some measure four inches), and they contrive to totter about on them in quite a lively manner.

The only Christian member of that household is one of the younger daughters, towards whom I felt very tenderly, thinking how she must need

God's grace to help her take up her cross daily, and follow the Master amid such surroundings.

Can we, in our favored land, estimate the trials of their faith, who in the midst of heathenism set out upon the heavenly race? Oh, how I longed to speak a word of encouragement to her; to tell her that we were fellow pilgrims, and remind her of the "crown of life, which the Lord hath promised to them that love Him," when in His strength they have endured this world's temptations! I might have asked Faith to be my interpreter, but she was talking with some one else, and I could not interrupt her.

With many friendly handshakings we took our leave, feeling sure that our visit had been a great diversion to the monotonous lives of the Chinese ladies in their boudoirs, so stiff and unattractive with stone-paved floors, hard chairs, and high latticed windows that afford no glimpse of the plebeian world.

Mr. Duncan had returned to Hong Kong on learning Arthur's intention of joining us. We found him in Mrs. Worthington's parlor when we arrived there, hot and tired after our interesting call. With great satisfaction I presented to Faith the brother whose name she had heard at least one hundred times since we came to Canton.

At the tea-table, when we had stopped laughing over Marion's description of the Minquas' unique style of entertaining their callers, Mr. Worthington said to his daughters, "You must take our friends over to Shameen before they leave us. Why not go this evening?"

Every one was quite willing to visit "Shameen," an island where reside the foreign merchants whom business brings to Canton. It is separated from the city by the narrow canal before alluded to, and its grass and trees are refreshing objects in view from the Worthingtons' windows; still, more so were they when, having crossed the canal by a bridge, we found ourselves away from the noisy, dirty city, and in cool seclusion. There is a little Episcopal church in Shameen, and the low-roofed bungalows, or loftier buildings with arched verandas, are occupied chiefly by bachelors who live in luxury that many of their sex might envy — no wives to make them give an account of their doings, no one to prevent them from smoking their very wits away, if they are so inclined, during the hours when the suspension of business leaves them to quiet enjoyment in their cane lounging chairs, contemplating through their verandas' arches the encircling Canton river, while the slow plashing of oars is uninterrupted by any gabble from the much dreaded female tongue.

"There is one merchant here who has a family," saith Faith, after alluding to the company of young bachelors, several of whom passed us as we strolled along the broad stone walk on the edge of the island.

"Are those ladies playing croquet, his wife and daughters?"

"No, they belong to the English mission. Come and be introduced, they will not mind the interruption."

We stood a few minutes on the croquet ground, and resumed our walk as the sun's last spark vanished. A bank of dark purplish clouds, overhanging the river, glowed with a crimson illumination that was reflected upon the white houses, and made our own faces seem almost unearthly to each other, as we sat down to feast our eyes on that sunset beauty.

"The remembrance of such evenings as this would make one feel almost cool in the crowded thoroughfares of yonder city," said Arthur. "Miss Faith, why do not you missionaries live over here, and get all the benefit of these rural surroundings?"

"We should not be so accessible here to the Chinese," Faith replied. "No Chinaman can cross the bridge without a pass, and however great the benefit of a residence among these trees might be to us, our work would suffer, for the people could not feel free to come to us at all times with their wants and woes as they do now."

"Who was the old woman I saw at your house to-day?" I inquired. "She had quite a different look from other Chinese women of her age, whose ugliness has appalled me. The wrinkled face of this one was kindly and loveable."

"She is one of the Bible readers employed by our Mission," said Faith, "and her history is very interesting. From the country, three hundred miles away, that woman came to Canton with her son, who is a paralytic, to seek medical treatment at the hospital. Their native dialect is the Mandarin, altogether unlike the Cantonese, but the written language being the same all over the Empire, was employed by the missionaries as the means of communication.

"It was through very little of man's teaching that the knowledge of salvation soon came to both mother and son. They read the Bible, and in their ready acceptance of its truth, we had a striking example of the power of the Holy Spirit as a teacher. The sincerity of their faith was severely tested when a rich uncle, upon whom they were dependent for support, sent word that if they joined the Christians he would do nothing more for them. They did not waver at this. After uniting with the Church, they both wanted to begin at once to serve their Lord by bringing other souls to Him.

"There is in the city a quarter where Mandarin-speaking people live, and the son begged the missionaries to get him a wheeling chair, in which he might push himself about the streets to tell his countrymen the gospel story. Such a thing could not be found here, but they hired a little room for him in the Mandarin quarter, where he lies on his couch ready to talk with any seeker after truth. His dear old mother goes through the streets, Bible in hand, to instruct all the women who will listen to her.

"Medical treatment has so far helped the young man that he can use his hands now, and father often employs him with writing. They have never been suffered to want food or shelter, and all the uncle's riches, I have heard them say, could never have brought them the true gladness of heart that the Lord Jesus gives to his followers. Their neighbors call them the 'happy people.'"

"That is interesting, indeed," said Arthur. "I am glad you told us their history, and sometime I may rehearse it at a missionary meeting; for it should lead other Christians, whose privileges are far greater, to consider why they are not all known as 'the happy people.' In giving the paralytic and his mother this title, their heathen acquaintances unconsciously echo the Psalmist's words, 'Yea, happy is that people whose God is the Lord.'"

We stayed at Shameen until a late hour, drifting in the course of conversation from China to America, relapsing occasionally into long pauses, when the murmur of the water against the stonework and the chirp of wakeful crickets, or a call from some passing boatman were the only sounds to break the quiet of the starlight, and the Great Dipper, rising slowly in the sky, warned us that

Saturday night was drawing near the first hours of Sunday. My story of Canton would be incomplete if I omitted to tell you anything of our Sunday there. Will your patience be equal to a description of one more day?

Services were held in a large room on the lower floor of Mr. Worthington's house, and about seventy-five Chinese converts were present, besides several missionary families. One Chinaman united with that little company of believers, and while the Confession of Faith and the Covenant were read, he stood up to signify his acceptance of them.

Marion whispered to me, "Notice the expression of his face."

It had already caught my attention, and I remembered, as I knew she did, an assertion of Lieut. Neufville's that no Chinaman was ever truly converted. He was not a remarkably fine-looking man, but as he stood before the pulpit with head erect and a beaming face, I said to myself that, whatever all the world might try to

One of Faith's Scholars. — Page 185.

prove to the contrary, nothing would persuade any one who had seen that convert that he did not realize what he was doing, and did not feel that he had come "out of darkness into marvellous light."

Faith Worthington has two girls' schools under her superintendence, and we visited them with her that Sunday afternoon. There seemed to be in each of them almost as many large girls and women as children. The mothers often come in, we were told, to hear their children recite. One at a time they advanced, these little yellow maidens, and making a reverence to their teacher, immediately turned their backs to her, and commenced their recitation of lessons from the Bible, and from a simple catechism. What appeared to us the height of rudeness was in them only a common civility, for to face a teacher while reciting would be an absolute insult to her, according to the Chinese code of etiquette. Then followed the singing of tunes most familiar to us: — "There is a Happy Land," "Jesus, lover of my soul," etc., with words that had any thing but a euphonious sound, and in all sorts of keys, while Faith's strong, clear tones rose above the others, as she tried to lead them into some degree of harmony. The words of the first-mentioned tune were somewhat as follows:

> "Cum yau yat shaw fuk da,
> Tsoi u un fong.
> Sheun do u wing chung ka,
> U yat che kwong.

After the singing came a little preaching from Faith, who sat still in her chair, bending forward slightly in her earnestness, her deep eyes fixed lovingly upon the faces of her hearers, while she discoursed in Chinese with a fluency that I never knew her to equal in English. Some of the children looked very apathetic, some wore an expression of suffering (and those had their feet bound in the painful manner necessary to the formation of a genteel shape), and a few bright little girls listened as if they dreaded to lose a word. I noticed among the women also those who were very attentive, if their expressions could prove it, and an emphatic nod of the head frequently bore witness of their inward convictions that the teacher was telling them "all truth and no lies," as one of them said to her.

In the evening there were services in the house where we had dined, at the other side of the city, and being rather tired, we went there in a sampan. Afterwards we walked home in a procession. Arthur and Mr. Worthington escorted some of the elder ladies. Faith, Marion, and I, preceding them, had opportunity for a long talk, our last in Canton, and Agnes, bearing a lantern, led the way through the dark streets, which at that late hour were almost deserted. With her sweet, innocent face framed by shining curls, her dress made dazzlingly white by the rays of light which enveloped her, she looked like some pure little spirit sent to guide mortals through the gloomy and devious ways of earth.

Marion opened her heart to Faith on the subject of missons, telling her that every thing seen and heard in Canton had increased her reverence for the work and the workers; then she brought up the subject of her conversation with Lieut. Neufville, confessing that she wanted some of his cavillings answered by Faith's wisdom, — not so much to satisfy her own mind, as to give her a more clearly defined idea of what might be said in future to such people.

"My dear, it would need more wisdom than I possess, to reply to the criticisms and objections of those who have no interest in missionary labors," said Faith. "But what did this Lieutenant say?"

"Well, first of all he said missionaries were always quarelling among themselves 'like cats and dogs,'" said Marion, suddenly growing dumb with consternation at the idea that she might have wounded Faith by the suggestion.

"That certainly is not true in Canton," quietly replied the young advocate of missions, "and is far from being the rule elsewhere. However, I am grieved to say that I have sometimes heard of disagreements among them, and what does it prove? That we are all erring human beings, yet perhaps no worse than our Lord's disciples, who, even in His sacred presence, disputed who should be the greatest. We dishonor His cause and our high calling when we follow their example, but He did not dismiss them from His service as being unfit for it, but endued them with His Spirit, who helped their infirmities, and allowed them to become the teachers of the world; and must our work be held as of no account because the workers are imperfect? What next, Marion?"

"Objections second and third were that the heathen are well enough as they are, believing in their own gods, and they will not be punished for not believing what they never heard of."

"The latter thought involves a deep mystery," said Faith; "yet Paul seems to recognize the lost condition of the heathen when he says, 'Whosoever shall call upon the name of the Lord shall be saved. How then shall they call on Him in whom they have not believed? and how shall they believe in Him of whom they have not heard? and how shall they hear without a preacher? and how shall they preach except they be sent?'

"Just here is the argument for the necessity for foreign missions. Did Christians universally recognize this, millions of money would be poured into the treasury, and thousands of laborers would offer themselves for the work.

"We are, however, told that the servant who knew not his Lord's will, and did it not, shall be judged differently from those who were enlightened.

"But how can we fathom the profound question of the heathen's responsibility? It is enough, I believe, to be sure they are in the hands of a God who cannot deal unjustly, and He has given a great many of those whom I know, a clearer idea of right and wrong than is generally considered belonging to the heathen.

"As to their faith in their own gods, we know that in a great number it is a very weak faith, and has no power to make them happy, or to elevate them in any way. Lately a poor woman said to me, 'I was sure the heart inside of me was very dark and evil, my sins were like a burden. When I prayed to my gods I did not feel they could hear or help. Long years ago, some white lady told me of one she called Jesus, who came to bear away these heavy sin burdens, and I never quite forgot the story, though it was very dim in my thoughts. Then you came and told me the rest, all of it, and I pray to Him, and that big burden is taken away from me, so I will pray always to Him to help me go in the right way.'"

We walked on silently for a time, until Faith inquired if Marion remembered any more of the officer's objections.

"One was that a Chinaman never was known to be truly converted; but, dear Faith, I know better than to agree with that declaration. What I have seen and learned in Canton contradicts it sufficiently without any pains on your part, although you told me once that the missionaries are sometimes deceived in those who were considered converts."

"John speaks of such in his First Epistle," I added. "'They went out from us, but they were not of us.' In other lands than China we find those who are professors of the faith, without being partakers of it."

"Finally," Faith said, "I might close the question by quoting the words of the Duke of Wellington, which contain, I think, the substance of the whole matter, and the decisive argument for foreign missions.

"It is said that he once met a young clergyman who, being aware of the Duke's former residence in the East, and his familiarity with the ignorance and superstition of the natives, proposed the following question: 'Does not your Grace think it almost useless and extravagant to preach the gospel to the Hindoos?' The Duke immediately replied, 'Look, sir, to your marching orders: *Preach the gospel to every creature.*"

"Oh, dear girls!" Faith went on to say, "the only thing to be considered is our Master's command, and in obeying it we do not depend on seeing great results, — they are in His hands; but even to help one soul find peace in believing we consider worth living here for. My little blind girl said to me one day, 'Dear teacher, my life is a new one since I believed what you told me about our Heavenly Father and the Lord Jesus;' and the death-bed of another scholar showed all her heathen relatives that she had a hope that could do for her what none of theirs could; it made her say, as she clasped my hand, 'I feel He is with me. It is all bright."

Our walk had ended, and we stood by the canal for a moment as Faith ceased to speak, her face radiant as she turned it towards us. We took her hands in ours, saying, by one impulse: "Truly you do have, even in this life, the 'hundred fold!'"

Now I really have no more to say about Canton, except that we left it the next day, with a promise from Faith that she would take a little rest and recreation by coming to Hong Kong for a visit on the "Lyra" before a fortnight should pass by.

We have resumed our gay harbor life, and each day brings new diversions. We receive a great many calls, and are invited to dinner or tiffin on steamers, go to see captains' wives who are our neighbors in the harbor, ride about the city in sedan chairs to do our shopping, and take rowing lessons in the evening under the auspices of Mr. Fordyce, or the first mate, or Arthur, when he is not playing the agreeable host to some skipper. Brass buttons honor us frequently; the "Ariadne" officers really seem to have missed us while we were away, and are now making up for lost time. But with all our gaieties, I do not think we are quite the same girls who trod the "Lyra's" deck two weeks ago. Our glimpse into the heart of heathendom, and into lives of such high and steadfast aim as those we have seen, could hardly fail to have a deepening influence, even upon the most frivolous character.

Write us all about everything and everybody at home; that will make a letter equal in length to this.

Yours with true friendship,

AMY.

CHAPTER VIII.

RETURN TO HONG KONG.

MARION'S STORY.

Hong Kong Harbor, June 31, 18—.

GUSSIE, MY DEAR FRIEND,—I am a sadder and a wiser girl than when my last letter to you was written. This harbor life of ours, though decidedly picturesque, has its dark side. Wherein the darkness lies I will explain by informing you of some grave facts.

People out here are not what they seem; appearances are deceitful (especially the appearance of navy officers); and I might add that there is neither truth nor virtue in mankind, were it not for a few who would be living contradictions to such a sweeping assertion.

Another fact is that we are tired of Hong Kong, for the heat is intense, and that, or something, disagrees with us all, and there is no longer novelty in any object around us; even the passing of a junk seems hardly more remarkable than that of a horse-car at home. We pine to set sail for Manila, and must continue to pine until the price of hemp falls, and the "Lyra's" owner deems it for his interest to purchase a cargo of it at the Philippines. Meantime we remain here and have dyspepsia, even indicati̇̇ of cholera, or else go home by one of the P̧. Mail steamers, and ingloriously give up our voyage around the world. A hopeful prospect, isn't it? We will turn from it while I look back over the past six weeks, and give you their history.

At this point you are wondering if Faith Worthington made us a visit, and I am happy to tell you that the dear girl came down in the

Canton boat early in June to stay awhile. She was charmed with everything on board our ship; even with the state-room of six feet by four allotted to her.

"It is all so queer!" she said, surveying the pink-curtained berth, and the little square window, through which numerous mast-heads were visible against the evening sky. "Here you seem as much at home as if you had never lived in a house, while I feel like somebody in a dream — not my own self at all."

"That's right," said Amy; "lose your identity for a while, and you will go home to your work all the fresher."

She didn't look like one who needed freshening as she stood before my small cracked looking-glass, brushing out a mass of shining hair and talking merrily to us; yet sometimes I could see a weary look in the blue eyes, and I felt sure a week of fun was just what she ought to have.

"Come up on deck now, and enjoy the sunset and breeze. After tea we will admit you into

Return to Hong Kong. 199

our boat club, if you are not tired, or else you can go as passenger."

Faith much preferred to take an oar. When the moon had risen, we seated ourselves in the "Skimmer" with Mr. Fordyce, and rowed to Wanchi, the lower end of the harbor, resting often to have a song and look about us. The mountains were reflected in the glassy water, and the city lights at the base of Victoria Peak multiplied themselves in the clear, mirror-like surface. We passed under the bow of many a stately vessel, glancing up at the sailors, who leaned over to watch our boat with its crew of three hatless girls, dressed in airy muslins, and a steersman who lounged tranquilly in the stern.

"What is it, Faith?" we asked, as a subdued ripple of laughter broke from her.

" A remark in Chinese, not intended for our ears, from a Chinaman on the ship we just passed. He told his companion to notice 'those three foreign devil-women down there rowing that boat!'"

"The miserable pagan!" said Mr. Fordyce. "Any other kind of man would have observed in awe, 'See those sylph-like forms, resembling in their white draperies the fleecy clouds that sail above us;' but gallantry cannot be expected from a Chinaman. Now, my fair oarswomen, let us go over to that flag-ship the 'Delaware,' and listen to her band for a few happy moments. I know you don't mean to put an end to my present rapture by rowing back to the 'Lyra' now."

The "few happy moments" lengthened into a good half-hour while we floated around the "Delaware," listening to the dreamy strains of music, and it was with a start that we finally resumed our oars when two bells (nine o'clock) sounded from a neighboring vessel. With steady strokes we pulled over the half-mile to the "Lyra" — no more resting and romancing that evening — and our haste was not in vain, for Captain Arthur stood at the gangway, saying in a tone of relief, "Here you are at last, and six callers have been waiting on board for nearly an hour!"

They were all navy officers, the "Ariadne" trio and some of their friends from an English man-of-war, the "Brunswick." I did hope, after all Faith had heard of Lieut. Neufville, that she would have a chance of talking with him, and so it undoubtedly would have been, had not one of the Englishmen, Lieut. Surrey, engrossed her completely all the evening. Before they took their leave an excursion to the top of the Peak was planned for the next day.

That night was the first of a series in which we have "camped out" on deck, for the heat is intolerable in our state-rooms, and three "cots" (like hammocks, only shaped so that berth mattresses fit into them) that were sent us from the "Ariadne" are hung under the awning, and in these swinging beds we repose during the first half of the night, usually going below before a glimmer of dawn appears.

On the night in question, I did not sleep much, for radiant moonlight flooding the harbor and mountains made the scene so lovely that I did not wish to close my eyes upon it, — neither did I wish to be oblivious of the presence of Faith in the next cot; therefore I lay with my head hanging over the side of my cot, looking at and talking too her till long after midnight.

The next day, June 10th, will long be a memorable one in my calendar. It was hot enough, I thought at the time, to be remembered only for that reason; but there have been many days since then quite equal to it in that respect. At the Praya landing we met our naval escort, Lieut. Gaines, Mr. Caulkin, and Lieut. Surrey of the "Brunswick."

Captain Arthur aud Mr. Fordyce were of the party, and as every one of us had to engage four coolies with a chair for the steep ascent, a goodly number of people that afternoon wound slowly up the narrow mountain path. Little streams came rushing down to meet us, and goats were feeding on their grassy borders. With every turn of the path the view became wider, and it made Amy almost dizzy to look below upon the city roofs, as she reflected that a stumble of her bearers might easily send her rolling down to them. Such catastrophes do not easily occur to me when I am having a good time, and when we came to a notch in the mountain chain where a glimpse of sea view began to be visible, and I was told that the tall post by the way had been erected in memory of an English traveller, killed on the spot by Chinamen, it didn't trouble me, though a thought glanced through my mind that we white people were only seven, three of us girls, and if our twenty-eight Chinese bearers felt like having a massacre then and there, how could we help it? I dismissed the unprofitable conjecture at once.

Arriving at last at the summit of Victoria Peak, we had a grand view;—on one side the familiar harbor with its fleet, and the many-tinted hill on the mainland;—on the other the blue ocean, glittering in the June sunbeans, numberless islands, and the Yat-moon pass, through which the "Lyra" had been guided so safely; and a bracing salt wind refreshed us, as it used to in the days before we came to China and felt its burning heat. With the wind, and a rush of feeling occasioned by the panorama, I was speechless and sat down in the long grass at the very edge of the precipice, with a heart almost oppressed by a revelation of beauty such as my eyes had never seen before. Faith and I, though very unlike in character, seem to think and feel at times as if one spirit moved us, and she sat down suddenly, just as I did, overcome by the same emotion.

Mr. Caulkin regarded us with astonishment, which was shared by Lieutenant Surrey. "I thought you would be perfectly delighted at this view," he cried, "and there you sit without a word to say — so coolly that we might imagine you had lived up here a month."

"Do you want us to give one shriek and roll over this green precipice?" I inquired. "Because *my* present feelings can be manifested in no other way, and if we keep from such an expression of them there is no use in attempting words." He did not understand us at all, it was evident, and went to borrow a spy-glass from the man who has a little house on Victoria Peak, and raises the signal flag when steamers enter the harbor, perhaps deluding himself with the belief that we needed some aid of that sort to our enthusiasm. I had no ambition to discover the occupations of people on the vessels far below us, as some of the others amused themselves by doing. All such things seemed trifling when that grand and varied picture attracted the eyes.

Captain Elton, one of our neighbors in the harbor, used his spy-glass to advantage that afternoon, for he told Mr. Duncan he had seen two of the young ladies sitting on the grass at the edge of the Peak, with a curious-looking shawl wrapped around them both. It was the German flag that Arthur folded us in when the sea-breeze grew too cool, and Amy, enveloped in a small edition of the stars and stripes, sat there also, while they compared her to the Goddess of Liberty. Mr. Surrey's position was on a rock by the side of Miss Worthington, and it would appear, even to the careless observer, that the impression made by her on his mind and heart was very different from any that one of her sex had produced before. He had walked more than halfway up the mountain by the side of her chair, leaving his own empty, and I could not help hearing snatches of their conversation, which turned on missions; but it was not a sober talk at all, for he asked the most ridiculous questions, and expressed so openly his wonder that she could really want to live among the heathen and teach them, when she might have stayed in America and led the gay life of a young lady in New York or Philadelphia society, that Faith's sense of amusement at him interfered with serious replies, such as she would naturally have given under other circumstances.

As we were resting on the Peak he renewed the attack in the same bantering strain, and in reply to her smiling assurance that she really loved her work, and would not give it up for any gaities to be enjoyed in America, he drew a long breath in despair of understanding a girl who entertained such sentiments, and reiterated, "Well! I don't see, for the life of me, how you can find any pleasure in teaching these dirty little heathen. It is beyond me!" Faith looked at him gravely, as if she quite believed it was beyond him, and felt sorry that it was so. To enter then before six people into the motives that impel and direct her happy life of service did not seem easy to her, I knew; yet when she thinks her "banner" should be "displayed because of the truth," it goes mightily against the grain for her to be silent. Arthur saw and understood her troubled expression, and answered in her behalf, "Miss Worthington is true to her name, for you know, my dear Surrey, that Faith looks beyond things temporal to those that are unseen and eternal."

The Lieutenant was silent, and Mr. Fordyce

looked up quickly with something in his handsome face that I never saw there before. A ray of light had come to him, perhaps, upon a subject hitherto hidden in darkness.

As I do not mean to keep your imagination fixed too long on the summit of Victoria Peak, it is time for me to invite it to descend, as we did, toward the sea, into a sort of basin of the mountains, around which their furrowed green sides rose high above us. The coolies stopped to drink at an impetuous little stream that gurgled out of a rocky gorge, and we alighted to try our pedestrian powers. Passing Douglas Castle, a mysterious building that would call to your mind some of Walter Scott's descriptions if it were grey and old-looking as it ought to be, we came at last into a smooth, level road, walled on the right by masses of rock, half-hidden by a wild growth of vines. On the left stretched the ocean, dyed crimson by the setting sun, and when that bright hue had faded, the moonlight flashed from the waves, and made startling shadows of our advancing sedan-chairs and their bearers.

By that time we had resumed our seats, and the Chinamen who bore the feminine portion of the company, not finding themselves heavily burdened, were proceeding at a pace that left the more substantial riders far in the rear — a state of things that alarmed us, for that part of the city called China-town was before us, and no unprotected girl would be willing to pass through it after dark. The pidgin-English command " man-man " (stop or walk slowly) was given with ineffectual earnestness, and we implored Faith to try the power of their own tongue upon the coolies. In vain were her Chinese remonstrances; they replied, not at all respectfully, that they were hungry, — wanted their suppers, — would go as fast as they pleased; and on they trotted, while behind us the gentlemen, in consternation that equalled our own, urged on their tired Chinamen to overtake us. They did so with difficulty just before we entered the city, and Lieut. Surrey handed Faith his umbrella that she might "hang on to one end," as he said, while his hand, retaining the other, prevented another separation. Amy and I were closely attended by the other escorts to the Praya landing, where our patient boat-boys had been waiting for an hour, and we promised the officers that we would give them a New England supper of baked beans, and afterwards row them to the "Ariadne;" — a rash promise, accepted by them, but the last clause unfulfilled by us, who realized when at last resting in the "Lyra's" cabin how weary we were.

A caller from the city was there to see Faith — a youth whose acquaintance she had made during a voyage from San Francisco to China eight months before. (I think Amy or I must have mentioned to you that she went to America at the age of thirteen, to spend four years at school, and returned only last summer.) This individual is hardly old enough for a young man, or young enough for a boy; he is more intelligent and gentlemanly than two-thirds of the people one meets in travelling round the world, and his surname is Payne. We know him well enough to call him Dick by this time, and have charitably adopted him for a younger brother, our hearts being touched by his evident homesickness in the uncongenial atmosphere of Hong Kong society.

Oh, this is the stiffest of places! The English are on the top rounds of the ladder; the rich Americans, a little below them, put on even more airs than they do; while those who do business on a small scale are very far down, and have to keep to themselves. Dick is only a clerk, and a very young one, so he is much to be pitied in a city where people are not judged by their own worth.

After one week, into which was crowded more festivity that I can tell you of now, we watched the Canton steamer out of the harbor, while our friend's face and figure in the stern faded from our sight, as she went back to resume her work.

We felt it was probably a final parting as to this present world, but remembering the words of a German princess, "Christians never part for the last time," we wiped away a little mist from the eyes that followed the steamer, and said to each other that it was a good thing to have known her, and we would always be grateful for that privilege. I wish the same could be said of even half a dozen among our numerous acquaintances in the city and harbor, and then my youthful mind might not learn such bitter lessons as are constantly forced upon it. Don't laugh, Gussie, I tell you it is no laughing matter to be disappointed in nearly everybody you like, and to find that however prepossessing may be their appearance and manners in your society, away from it their actions are not such as a right-minded woman could approve. I believe some girls say they do not object to young men being "a little fast!" Do you suppose they have any idea of what they are talking about? If people could be "fast" in the right direction no one could reasonably object, but my experience of fastness assures me that it is more apt to be connected with a turn to the left.

In these days we see no more flashes of brass buttons upon our gang-way steps, except when Lieut. Surrey haunts us of an evening to inquire "the latest news from Canton." A misunderstanding with one of the " Ariadne " officers created a coolness which affected his friends also, and they dropped us without giving us a fair chance to explain the cause of an act of seeming rudeness, quite unintentional on the part of Amy and myself. We were not deeply grieved on account of this desertion, though sorry to be considered unladylike by any one.

Dick Payne spends nearly every evening on the " Lyra," thankful to escape from the torrid climate of the city when his office work is done, and often Mr. Duncan and he row us to Kowloon, as the land opposite Hong Kong is called — a lonely place, where we ramble over the slopes, or rest on some glassy bluff that rises steeply above the beach where the water ripples break, while crickets chirp around us, and across the harbor gleam the lights of the city which Dick emphatically wishes might be swallowed by an earthquake before his eyes, rather than he should be forced to return to it. His kind heart would repent of the wish if he saw any chance of it coming to pass; but he is the most homesick boy I ever tried to console.

Last night, for variety, we rowed over to Stone-cutters' Island just before sunset, taking our supper with us, and Arthur was easily persuaded to be one of the party. Rocks, grass, a deserted garden where weeds and tropical fruit-trees grow in rank abundance, and a stone jail form the unattractive features of this island, and a more forlorn place than it must be in the noon-day glare I cannot imagine; yet a sunset of real watermelon hue softened its naturally forbidding aspect and gave to the jail the look of a picturesque old castle. We went into it, of course, all being curious creatures, and were surprised to find some of the English missionaries, who said they had come there to take up their abode for a few days. Although they did not occupy cells, but cool, large rooms, it seemed a preposterous idea that any one could find an agreeable change and recreation in a jail; but Hong-Kongites will do a good deal for a breath of fresher air than can be had under those oppressive mountains that stand so near the city.

Our repast was spread out on a flat rock by the beach, and the delicate question of the best way to open a box of sardines gravely discussed. We knew they would not be good for us, but none the less was our determination to enjoy them. Arthur settled it by putting the box up on a rock endwise, and firing his pistol at it; — result, a round hole in the box, and the contents poked out with a penknife in the form of sardine hash!

"After all," it is said during these pleasant evenings, "we are not so very miserable, even if we can't set sail for Manila." When the next morning comes, though, with its relentless stare of sunshine, and Victoria Peak seems to perspire in the region of its rocky brow, and we lie listlessly in cane lounging-chairs, trying to quench our thirst with that insult to the palate called "congee" (thin rice-water), dosing ourselves at intervals with "Brown's Cholera Mixture"— then is the time to say—"Must this state of things last through August if our owners won't send us to Manila? Or shall we go home by the Pacific mail?"

There are two visitors besides Dick who remain faithful to us. One is an elderly doctor, whose liking for Amy brings him on board so often that warlike feelings are excited in her mind when Mr. Fordyce calls up from the lower deck, about once a day, "Miss Amy, I see the doctor's boat coming." The other is still more elderly, a white-haired, delightful gentleman, named Dowling, who is connected with one of the largest mercantile houses here, and used to know Uncle Roslyn when he lived in America.

A few evenings ago he brought a young friend to take tea with us, Captain Harold Fay of the steamer "Suwanee," and we were greatly pleased to find him a native of Boston, and so earnest in his affectionate regard for his home, as he still considered it, that to talk about its streets and people seemed a real satisfaction to him. His steamer leaves this harbor for Singapore on the 3rd of every month, touching at Saigon, a French port in Cochin-China, on the way. After enlarging upon the tropical beauties of Singapore, he turned to me, saying, " You and Miss Roslyn ought to take a trip there with me before you leave China;" to which I replied in the most commonplace words, " It would be very pleasant if we could."

" Oh! wouldn't it?" said Amy, after the gentlemen had gone ashore, echoing my words, as I repeated them more emphatically than when answering Captain Fay. " It would cost ever so much," was one obstacle, and another, suggested by Arthur, " Of course, I couldn't let you girls go alone, neither ought I to leave the ship for a month to go with you."

"Well, don't let us think about it, for it is too tantalizing," and we dropped the subject.

I have a feeling that something is going to happen to us next month — not a voyage to Singapore, for the "Suwanee" sails in two days, and there is no prospect of the obstacle I mentioned being removed — but *something:* an order to proceed to Manila, or a departure for America in the next steamer. I hope it will not be the latter, whatever it is, for it would be far better to stay here all summer and be scorched, than to give up our journey round the world. Don't you think so?

CHAPTER IX.

SAIGON AND SINGAPORE.

AMY'S STORY.

*Steamer "Suwanee," China Sea,
Aug. 30th.*

DO you wonder, Gussie, that you do not see the familiar name of Hong Kong Harbor at the head of this letter? Are you saying to yourself, "What has befallen those girls now?" Something remarkable, be assured, for we have visited Singapore, and are now steaming back to our harbor-home after nearly a month's absence.

Marion's last effusion was a kind of wail, was it not? and if I had written in July according to my feelings, you would have received one of yet more doleful cadence; but no gilded vane on church steeple ever veered more suddenly than did those same feelings on the 2nd day of August when, hot and miserable, I was fanning myself on the sofa in the captain's office, and was electrified by these words as Arthur entered:

"Amy! Marion! Hurry and pack your trunk, for the 'Suwanee' sails at three this afternoon, and you are going to Singapore in her by invitation of Mr. Dowling."

Cinderella was not more pleased when her fairy godmother turned a pumpkin into a coach to take her to the ball, than we were with this welcome invitation. It seems that the dear old gentleman, meeting Arthur in Queen's Road, said, "I was just on my way to the 'Lyra,' for the notion of going to Singapore with Fay has seized me, but I don't care about it unless you will let those girls of yours go with me. I'll take wonderful care of them." Captain Roslyn could have no doubt of that, so he did not demur at the

Saigon and Singapore. 221

prospect of a month's loneliness for himself, but came to give the announcement that startled us both into an excited packing of one small trunk, and before the sun went down the Peak was far out of sight, and we were on the wide ocean once more; standing in the "Suwanee's" bow with a cool salt wind blowing even the remembrance of heat away from us, and every prospect of a good time ahead. In a steamer that one might suppose to have been built expressly to afford pleasure trips to a few passengers, conveniently arranged and handsomely fitted up; her captain an unusually agreeable person when "so disposed;" with a kind, fatherly friend, who made us feel that we were conferring instead of receiving a favor by the acceptance of his invitation; sailing down the China Sea, serenely blue all day, and silvered after twilight, toward the land of palms, and revelling in anticipation of tropical beauty to be enjoyed there, — could we have dreamed of any better way than this of passing the month of August?

There were only three or four passengers beside our party, and we did not see much of any of them except a Mr. Leroy, who by reason of his excessively lively character, and information gathered from almost every clime, is well fitted for a steamer companion. His powers of entertainment, added to those with which Captain Fay is endowed; a large collection of stereoscopic views belonging to the latter; his photograph albums, from whose pages many a Boston face looked up at us with a pleasant surprise, and Cameron's book on Singapore were the charms that made three days slip away too quickly.

On the third day land was visible, — a long range of hills in the distance, which the captain said was the coast of Cochin China. We entered the Saigon River the next forenoon, passing Cape St. James, a thickly wooded promontory at its mouth, and for several hours were tracing its serpentine curves among shores covered with a low jungle growth. At five P.M. the "Suwanee" ran aground, and there was nothing to do but to wait patiently for two hours until the tide turned, and then we steamed up to the city. Not much of Saigon was to be seen in the hazy moonlight, and we retired to suffer the disturbance of swarms of mosquitoes in our state-room and of heathen outside the window, so there was little rest for us that night. Daylight revealed a view of vessels at anchor all around us; junks and sampans of patterns diverse from those with which we had become familiar in Hong Kong, huts of Chinese or Malays along the river banks, and some respectable buildings, the most inposing of them being the Messageries Imperiales, — the headquarters of French authority. Marion's attempt at sketching a thatched shanty under some palm trees was interrupted by a call from Captain Fay to join me in making the acquaintance of the mangosteen, "the queen of East India fruits," he called it, "and one that you will never know when to stop eating after you once taste it." She came reluctantly, asking if mangosteens were at all like magnos, for she has never conquered her aversion for that fruit, and persists in saying it has a turpentine flavor.

"No more like them than peaches are like watermelons," Mr. Leroy assured her, showing us a box of them, and producing plates and knives.

The first time one tastes a mangosteen is an epoch in the history of a life. It is about the size and shape of an apple, and has a hard dark shell which is crimson on the inside, and contains a pure white fruit, divided into lobes, and very juicy. The flavor is unlike any other in the world, I believe, therefore I cannot describe it; but Marion's face, as she swallowed one lobe and rolled up her eyes, then closed them with a sigh that told of rapture too deep for utterance, would have convinced any one of the mangosteen's virtue.

"You won't look so serene when I give you a dourian to eat," said Capt. Fay, who had observed her quizzically.

"When you drive around Singapore and judge

Saigon and Singapore. 225

by a certain odor greeting your olfactories that deceased cats and dogs are somewhere in the neighborhood, or that a breeze is wafted to you from the jungle where decaying elephants and tigers"—

"Stop these odorous comparisons, I beg," exclaimed Mr. Leroy.

"You needn't listen," responded the captain; "I will proceed to inform Miss Gilmer that under such circumstances she may know herself to be near a pile of dourians exposed for sale outside of some shop."

"Can people eat such things? What do they look like?"

"They are larger than a cocoanut, and have a green husk or shell; the interior is like a rich custard, and much appreciated by people who can overcome their disgust at the smell. The natives are very fond of them."

Mr. Leroy declared that he should send for a dourian before he had been in Singapore half an hour, and no perfume should deter him from eating one.

"We shall see," was the captain's skeptical reply.

Late in the afternoon we went ashore to see the wonders of Saigon, and in a queer little carriage rattled off to the Public Gardens — a place upon which the French people do not expend much labor in cultivation, and I liked it none the less for that. The straggling paths, winding among thickets of bamboo and palm, were rural enough, and pleased me better than if they had borne the marks of weeding and rolling. There were animals in cages there; some large tigers, one of whom when he saw us flew at his iron bars with such a roar of fury that Mr. Dowling drew me back involuntarily, as if he thought it could scarcely require more force to give the creature his freedom. Then we got into our carriage again and were driven over very good roads, edged with the greenest grass; past pretty, airy French houses, and the miserable hovels of the Chinese. Altogether, Saigon is a queer place; the French and Chinese elements do not seem to mingle well, and respectable buildings have a homesick look, — "as if they wished they were anywhere else on earth," Marion observed. There is a large Catholic nunnery there, but I did not see anything very attractive after we left the seclusion of the gardens, and we had no desire to go ashore again during the "Suwanee's" stay in the river. On the third day she steamed out to sea again, and our pleasant intercourse went on as before.

The captain grew more sociable every day, and seemed to find great delight in teasing Marion, and drawing her into discussions upon a variety of subjects. Another favorite pastime of this young man, whose dignified manners had once caused us to regard him with a degree of awe, was to address remarks and commands in pidgin-English to his steward, a very solemn Chinaman, at the dinner-table, for the apparent purpose of setting Marion into fits of laughter. Captain Fay's fluency in this tongue is so astonishing that the gravest person could not fail to be amused at listening to him, and Marion's strong sense of the ridiculous quite overcomes her. Sometimes we sit at the table from seven till nearly ten, so interested in conversation — not always nonsensical by any means — that we forget the attractions of the deck. One night Marion's declaration of the unbelief in mankind which residence in China has fostered in her heart, drew down upon her the captain's wrath, and when she enforced some of her statements by the avowal that our young adopted brother Dick was about the only person there in whom she had any real confidence, he was nearly dumb with a comical kind of indignation, and proposed an adjournment to the moonlight outside. There he renewed the strife, and feeling the need of some stimulant to support him in his arguments, he called for tea to be brought up on deck, and we all quaffed "the cup that cheers" with great enjoyment.

The fact is undeniable that none of us were in any hurry to get to Singapore; but early in the morning of August 13th, we passed among the outlying islands into a calm, wide bay, and drew up to one of the wharves at breakfast time. The captain took malicious pains to have a dourian brought to the table and placed before his friend Leroy, who had boastingly declared the strength of his purpose to eat one, despite its reputed odor. One whiff of it, which verified all Captain Fay had told us, caused Mr. Leroy to lean back in his chair, and recommend with rather a sickly smile that it should be exhibited to us through the cabin window, if the young ladies cared to make further inspection of it.

"Here steward," cried the captain, brimful of fun, but with a very grave exterior; "you takee him (the dourian); we no wantchee here — we makee look see him outside window," and the offensive dourian was conveyed to a distance.

In a "gharry," the Singapore hack, we rattled through the streets to the Clarendon Hotel, which stands in a lovely garden, fronting the bay. It seemed deserted by all its boarders, and we wondered, when summoned to tiffin in a great hall, that no one beside our three selves sat down at the table.

The reason was that there were no ladies staying there, and all the gentlemen were at their offices. At the seven o'clock dinner there was a formidable array of them, and when Marion and I left the table, each one pushed his chair back with a loud scrape on the uncarpeted floor and stood up, while we marched down the long room in much surprise and embarrassment, for we were not acquainted with English dinner-company etiquette, and had not been prepared for such a proceeding on the part of ten strangers.

One charm of these East Indian houses is a kind of verandah room furnished with cane lounging chairs, the floor covered with matting, and three sides of it open to the perfumed breezes. The parlor of the Clarendon Hotel leads into a retreat of this description, and there we spent the evening, looking through the white columns upon a tropical garden below us, and beyond its foliage to the quiet waters of the bay. We could hear the dash of a slow wave breaking at intervals on the sand, and behind one tall cocoanut palm a full moon shone gloriously. The effect was heightened by a sweet-tuned music box in the parlor, and through the half-closed door stole out to us the chimes of "Monastery Bells."

There was a boudoir connected with our room at the hotel, of which one whole side opened to the garden, and was shaded at will by Venetian blinds; and at seven o'clock every morning we partook of "chow-chow," brought there on a tray by a stately Kling, whose jet-black beauty was well set off by his snowy clothes and turban of striped scarlet and white cloth. Chow-chow in this case means a meal, not a pickle, and the term is generally applied to slight refreshment taken before the late breakfast. Crispy toast, fragrant tea, butter moulded into the semblance of a creamy rose, and thick slices of pine-apple that melt in the mouth, were the viands brought us by our Kling waiter; and who could resist such temptations, even when knowing they would take off the edge of an appetite for the substantial breakfast? We never attempted to resist, and the result was that afterwards curried chicken, and rice, and fried cakes were treated with indifference, and Mr. Dowling worried at our lack of appetite.

On Sunday morning we started to walk to the Scotch Kirk, persuading ourselves that we should not suffer from the heat; but we did, and were wishing for a gharry, when wheels sounded behind us, and from a carriage a young lady alighted, advancing with a frank, cordial manner to greet us, and introduced herself as the daughter of an elder in the Kirk.

"Are you going there?" she asked; "I thought it was probable, and also believed you must be the American strangers who I heard had come down with Captain Fay, and were

Saigon and Singapore.

staying at the Clarendon. I wish to save you the hot walk, if you will allow me the pleasure."

This good Samaritan, Miss Elsie Moore, not only conveyed us to the Kirk, but gave us a seat in her pew, and offered many thoughtful attentions, and after the services kindly responded to our request that she would call on us.

Mr. Dowling met an old friend of his in the porch, a Mr. Vane, who insisted that we should drive out of town to take tiffin with him, and we did so. One of the many smooth, shady roads that led out to the suburban residences, brought us to an elevated mansion with wide verandahs commanding a view of a distant hill-range, and there we had a light repast, and with conversation and sacred music passed away the hot hours of the day, driving into town in time for the service at the Episcopal church, just before dark. It was an elegant building, and the congregation was a very fashionable one, but a more formally conducted service I never attended, and I felt when it was over as if I had asked for bread and been given a stone. The fault may have been partly in myself, for I might have worshipped in God's house with a heart rising above coldly-read prayers, and a neat little moral essay of a sermon; yet after we passed out from those gothic arches, we went where my soul's craving was satisfied — and where was that, do you suppose? In the "Bethesda," an humble chapel where congregate that class of believers who call themselves "Brethren." They were not fashionable, and had neither minister nor choir. We all united fervently in singing such simple hymns as "Come to Jesus, just now"; and a lay brother at the desk gave us an affectionate, plain exhortation that bore out the spirit of those words. It seemed to me like the gatherings of the apostles in that "large, upper room," where, "with one accord, they continued in prayer and supplication;" and we drove back to the hotel feeling satisfied that we had made the most of our Sunday in Singapore.

The first thing that happened on Monday, was

The Esplanade. — Page 237.

Saigon and Singapore.

a call from a gentleman whose brother (now on a visit to Scotland) owns a fine cocoanut grove six miles out of town, to which he promised to drive us that afternoon; and he came for us in a comfortable barouche, greatly to our relief, after some forebodings of a ride in one of those noisy gharries. We drove about the town for a little while; down the Esplanade — a wide road that skirts the bay — seeing there several handsome buildings; then wound through the somewhat narrow and ill-paved, or paveless, business streets, where there seems to be nothing of nature's loveliness or of man's device to attract the eye; and round the corners come whiffs of the strongest dourian odor, until we were glad when the horses' heads were turned towards the country.

In one street the Chinese were holding a feast in honor of their departed ancestors. A long table was set out there, gaudily ornamented, and laden with their own peculiar delicacies for the benefit of those restless souls who, according to the popular belief, are continually demanding some attention on the part of their living relatives.

Our barouche rolled easily over a level road, bordered on either hand by crowds of tall cocoa palms, with little huts scattered about in the shade of their feathery leaves. After miles of this scarcely varied scenery, we turned into an avenue that led to the factories, where they make ropes out of the fibrous cocoanut shell, and oil from the nut. There were a good many long, low sheds, where the work was going on, and we alighted to inspect it, and strolled through the grove, eating pieces of the hard, white nut, slightly apprehensive that a whole one might at any time descend upon our heads from the tree-tops.

Our escort then said it must be nearly dinner-time, and we would drive to the house. I had expected to see an elegant mansion, where at least *one* lady would receive us; therefore, judge of my amazement when we alighted before a picturesque, though rather rough bungalow, where it appeared that our companion and a young man who has charge of the factories kept bachelors' hall, and the only invited guest beside Mr. Dowling and his girl *protéges* was the minister of the Kirk!

Dinner was served in a stone-paved room on the ground floor. A truly English round of beef, and oat cake as truly Scotch, were set before us, together with things that especially appertain to the tropics, and it was a very enjoyable repast, even if it did seem odd to have no hostess at the board. From an upper balcony afterwards we could see that for miles around were cocoanut trees — their plumy heads waving in the night breeze, and beyond them in one direction we could have had by daylight a far-off glimpse of the sea. Our drive back to the hotel was a dark one, for the trees that hemmed in the road were only far enough apart to show a narrow strip of the starry firmament above us, and in passing the thick jungle we wondered if tigers did not sometimes spring out of it upon late travellers like ourselves; but, leaning back on the carriage cushions, we were too drowsily comfortable to be much alarmed by any such surmises, and just before midnight we drove through the Clarendon gateway.

A few miles out of Singapore is the residence of a wealthy Chinaman by the name of Whampoa, and the garden around it is visited as a matter of course by all sightseers; so we were informed by Captain Fay, who made his appearance at our hotel the next afternoon with a friend of his, a Mr. Temple, saying briefly that he had a carriage at the door, and would take us to "Whampoa's Garden," unless we had something better to do. We had not, and ran with alacrity to put on our hats. On coming back to the verandah where the gentlemen were waiting, the captain handed us a letter from our Sunday acquaintance, Miss Elsie Moore, inviting us, in her mother's name, to dinner that evening.

"I am going," he informed us as I read it to

Marion and Mr. Dowling, "and so are Temple and Leroy. You must accept, for the Moores are charming people, and we shall be sure of a pleasant time."

"Of course," we replied, "but we can't go to a dinner-party dressed as we are now for a drive. You will have to wait fifteen minutes longer," and we wasted no time in arraying ourselves in evening costumes; then drove out to Whampoa's beautiful grounds.

It is a stiff beauty that reigns there, or it would not be truly Chinese. Straight, narrow alleys intersect the flower beds; box bushes trimmed into shapes of baskets, pagodas, and animals stand at every turn; long canals about three feet in width, are filled with lotus, whose rosy heads tremble on their slender stalks as if too heavy to hold up, and in a miniature lake we saw the Victoria Regia's great petals unfolded. It was not our expectation to enter the house, and we were the more pleased at receiving an invitation to do so from the proprietor, whom we met in the arbor, where he was exhibiting one of his pets, a huge six-legged turtle, to three gentlemen. Captain Fay knew these strangers, and presented us to Admiral Rodgers, and two captains from the United States frigate "Colorado," one being the captain of the fleet, the other of the frigate. We were also introduced to old Mr. Whampoa, a most courteous gentleman who speaks English well, and pressed us to walk into his house and take some refreshment. I was glad we had that opportunity, for the house is more remarkable than the garden, according to my judgment, and presents a singular combination of Chinese and English styles. One parlor opens into another by a great circular hole surrounded with openwork carving; costly rugs are spread upon the polished floors; marvels of ivory and sandal wood are scattered in profusion, and among furniture of unmistakably Chinese origin, the appearance of a few of such tables and chairs as you might see in any fine house in an American city causes one to feel

Page 242.

some surprise. Tea, cake, and wine were served, and we bade our host adieu with many thanks for his politeness. The stately, white-headed Admiral gave us an invitation to visit the "Colorado" on our return to Hong Kong, and told Mr. Dowling that she would soon follow the "Suwanee" there.

It was too dark when we reached the Moores' house to get much idea of its outer appearance, and it mattered little, for the inside was bright and homelike, and Miss Elsie's welcome dispelled all formality. Her father and younger sister greeted us kindly, and Mrs. Moore took our hearts captive at once. Her presence would make any one feel happier and better, and she is one, I think, to whom motherless girls, especially, must be drawn by some influence too sweet to be explained. Marion says, "It is just as if she spread out a great pair of wings and folded us under them." Our being thrown almost exclusively of late into the society of gentlemen made us appreciate in an unwonted degree what it was to sit down beside this dear motherly Scotch lady, and answer her questions of affectionate interest about our ship, our brother, the long sea voyage, and our distant home. I cannot say that a feast of reason prevailed at dinner, for we were all too jolly to be very sensible. Captain Fay and Mr. Temple, who were old friends of the Moores and very much at home, kept us in a state of merriment, and another guest, Mr. Fields, from Massachusetts, contributed to the general festivity. When dessert had received sufficient attention, Mrs. Moore arose, and we young females followed her out of the room like a brood of ducklings going after the parent bird, in accordance with the unprofitable custom of the ladies leaving the gentlemen to drink and smoke by themselves. These gentlemen did not appear to be winebibbers, however, for we were soon interrupted in a cosy chat over our coffee by their entering the parlor and proposing music. Every one sang or played, and we reflected no credit upon our instructors by our part of the performances; for, attempting to sing one of our duets, we made a grievous failure. Finally we Americans waxed patriotic and indulged in "The Star Spangled Banner," which merged into "The Bonnets of Blue," out of compliment to our entertainers, and a general uproar ended the evening.

On the day of our departure from Singapore Mr. Dowling noticed in one of the offices down town two large boxes of shells and coral — a great variety. He told the clerk that he should like to find a collection similar to this one for the young ladies who were travelling with him.

"These boxes are to go on board the 'Suwanee' to-day, sir," was the reply. "Mr. Fields intends them for Miss Roslyn and Miss Gilmer." Was not that a fine present?

Another reminiscence of Singapore was given me by the gentleman who took us out to the cocoanut grove — an alligator made of cork, frightfully natural, and ready to squirm his long tail at the slightest movement. It is the work of a Buddhist priest, I was told. After a few more drives and dinners, we took leave of that lovely land, and of those friends who had so greatly contributed to our enjoyment while there, and the "Suwanee" began her return trip on a bright August afternoon, receiving a salute from the noble "Colorado" as we passed her in the Bay. We were already on board the steamer when the "Catharine Apcar" from Hong Kong came up to the dock, and letters from Arthur and Dick Payne were handed to us just as the warning whistle sounded, and the last farewells were spoken. Naturally, we were gratified to learn how much they had missed us in our harbor-home, and were aided in realizing it by a pen-and-ink sketch entitled "Evenings on the 'Lyra' during the month of August, 1870." Four young men therein were represented as sitting in a row on deck, their feet up on the railing, expressions of extreme dejection on their faces, and cigars in the mouths of two, who appeared to be Dick and Mr. Fordyce. From Arthur's mouth issued these words: " Well; if I let my girls go away again without me — ! " and from Mr. Duncan's — " I daresay they will marry some one down there, and never come back." The artist of this touching group was not revealed in the letter, but we had cause to suspect the second mate. Marion executed a companion sketch to this, representing herself and me, with Mr. Dowling and Captain Fay on the deck of the steamer; each one of us comfortably extended in a bamboo reclining chair, and holding a tea cup — each face wearing a grin of unspeakable content, and Captain Harold exclaiming, as he stirred his smoking beverage, "Now this is domestic bliss — this is fine ! " Underneath was written " Evenings on the 'Suwanee' in the month of August, 1870," and we sent it to our lonely friends from Saigon, at which port we stopped again for a few days.

An English gentleman and his wife are the

only cabin passengers beside ourselves on this return trip. They are pleasant people, but quite reserved, and inclined to keep to themselves. The Captain and Mr. Dowling read aloud to us their favorite scraps of literature, and we spend our days on deck; our nights too, I might almost say, for midnight frequently finds us there — deep in conversation (and tea). Early tomorrow morning, if nothing happens to the "Suwanee's" machinery, she will come to her anchorage under the shadow of the Peak that we were so glad to leave a month ago, and shall be still more glad to see again, and be welcomed once more on the "Lyra."

P. S. from Marion. Sept. 5th. — I wouldn't let Amy send off her Singapore effusion without giving me a chance to tell you about some funny things that have happened since we got home. Oh! we had such a glorious time, .and such a welcome back! I don't write this postscript to tell you that, however, but to mention two adventures of ours in relation to the "Colorado." That grand flag-ship sailed into the harbor a few days ago, and Arthur made a prompt call on some of the young officers, inviting them to return civilities by a visit to the "Lyra," and little did he dream that they would come one afternoon when he had gone to the city and left his lambs without fraternal protection. Mr. Duncan, who was indulging in his favorite pastime of reconnoitering the harbor with a spyglass, started us all of a sudden by this announcement:

"I see one of the 'Colorado's' boats bearing down on us. It is full of officers — what will you do?" (this in a horrified tone, for he surely thought that ravening wolves were descending upon the fold in the absence of its guardian).

"Tell them the captain has gone ashore, and perhaps they won't come on board," said Amy, as we hurried down to the cabin so that they shouldn't be allured by white draperies, and waited there, quaking for fear of these unknown monsters. Mr. Duncan virtuously did as he was told in answer to their inquiries, and they were about to order their oarsmen to push off from the ship, when the irrepressible Fordyce added in a distinct tone, " The young ladies are aboard, sir."

"Oh, are they?" said the chief spokesman, "that's all right. Come along fellows, the girls are aboard," and up the gangway they clattered with as much noise as ten feet could make. Mr. Fordyce preceded them and handed us five visiting cards, a useless observance, for we didn't know who the names fitted, of course, and they all marched in before we had time to read them. In some remarkable manner the introductions were accomplished, and I barely kept myself from an explosion of laughter — the whole affair was so ludicrous. There were not chairs enough in the cabin for such an army of men, so we took them up on the house, and each of us had two and a half to entertain. No exertion on our part was needed, though; they entertained them-

Saigon and Singapore. 253

selves and us in the wildest style, flinging jokes and compliments around at random, and acting as if they had taken leave of their senses for a time, or at least had left them at a distance. It is probable that ardent spirits were influencing them, for if they had made several other calls that afternoon, and had accepted an invitation to partake of wine or brandy at every vessel, according to the doubtful habits of this place, it could not be wondered at that they should be a little beside themselves. No one expects Capt. Roslyn to treat them to anything alcoholic when they visit him, or if they do the first time they must be sadly disappointed, and never flatter themselves with that hope again. In the course of their conversational fire-works, they threw out an invitation for us to come to the next Sunday morning's service on their flag-ship, and promised us a "sermon of the first chop," adding as a still further inducement that they would sing "Shoo-fly" after it if we desired. As you may suppose, we did not respond to this with especial cordiality, and they soon departed, after a noisy leave-taking. Just picture to yourself Arthur's face when we told him all about it!

The real spice of the matter lies in the way we actually did visit the "Colorado," — not upon the invitation of these fast youths, but, as guests of that vessel's captains, whom we had met in Whampoa's Garden. Last evening we heard the clank of many oars in the rowlocks of some boat, and straightway Captain Fay appeared with one of the "Colorado" captains, to ask us to establish ourselves in the cushioned seats of a large boat rowed by twelve oarsmen, dressed in navy suits of white and blue. Arthur had a severe headache, and it seemed too bad for both of us to leave him, yet if one had stayed the other would have had to also, and he ordered us to go and have a good time.

"To the 'Plantagenet'" was the command given the rowers. "We will call for Miss Jennie Bryant," added Captain Fay to us. This young lady arrived in the harbor only a few weeks before we went to Singapore, in the course of a long voyage with her mother on the vessel which her father commands. Her intelligence and pleasing face and manners make her a general favorite — with sea-captains especially, on account of her nautical knowledge. I heard one of them say he would trust her to navigate a ship far sooner than many young officers.

With this addition to our company we drew near the "Colorado," and under her bulwarks listened to the familiar strains of "Swanee Ribber," which floated down from the quarter-deck where the band was playing; then we went on board. Two of our former acquaintances met us at the gangway steps, and gravely handed us to the deck; but the strict etiquette of the navy puts a barrier between the invited guests of a captain or an admiral and inferior officers like those flyaway sons of Mars; therefore, after decorously escorting us to the elegant quarters of their chiefs, they drew back, and we saw them no more. In such high company as that of the venerable Admiral did we spend the evening, and by him were we entertained. He showed us the pictures of his wife and daughters, saturated our handkerchiefs with the choicest cologne, and ordered refreshments to be served on the quarter-deck, where we sat so near the band that conversation was at a discount except in the pauses of the resounding brass. Such honors as these I have described must cause us forever to look down upon lieutenants and ensigns, except those who are *entitled* to respect by their solidity of character ; and where shall such be found ?

This, my dear, is a postscript worthy of the name, and I trust it will find an appreciative reader.

CHAPTER X.

SHANGHAI AND AMOY.

MARION'S STORY.

Hong Kong, Oct. 28th, 18—

SINCE the "Great Republic" carried away to American shores Amy's Singapore letter, with its addition of a postscript from my humble pen, two Chinese cities have been visited by your friends. We have been to Shanghai and Amoy, and as the train of circumstances which led to the trip may be considered somewhat remarkable, not to say romantic, I must open this month's history with a short preface.

While I was in California four of my friends at Mr. Clinton's school had a ferrotype group of themselves taken to send me. One of them was Jennie Greenough, who, as you will remember, has a married sister living in Shanghai.

When on the "Suwanee" I was showing my album to Captain Fay, and came to that ferrotype, I mentioned that fact as I told him who the girls were, asking if he had ever met Mrs. Ingraham. He said he knew her very well, and should see her in September, as business would then call him to Shanghai, and he knew she would be pleased to hear that a friend and schoolmate of her sister's was in Hong Kong. Several weeks passed, and I had almost forgotten that there was such a lady as Mrs. Ingraham, when a letter came from her, inviting me in most affectionate terms to visit her with my cousins; "for, to welcome one of Jennie's friends to my foreign home," she wrote, "would be only less gratifying to me than to see the dear little sister herself."

What could any one do under such circumstances but start directly for Shanghai, as we did in the steamer "Aphrodite?" Arthur left the "Lyra" to Mr. Duncan's faithful care for a fortnight, and went on the northward journey with his girls.

Our fellow-passengers were three in number — one solitary lady, who kept herself shut up, and two sociable gentlemen, one of whom, Captain Nichols, was a Hong Kong acquaintance. Our commander was Captain Croly, who would satisfy your ideal of a bluff, good-natured sailor, though you say Arthur does not, and I am sure Captain Fay is no nearer the mark. He used to pound on our state-room door in the morning, and in vociferous tones summon us to breakfast, "Come out this minute, girls! Now, don't be lazy;" then, to all who happened to be in the saloon, he would shout: "I believe they are both in a bad humor this morning; a fit of the sulks, perhaps;" which assertion never failed to bring us out with smiles that contradicted him.

The weather was clear and cool, and after dark it was hardly comfortable to be on deck, except while taking brisk walks in the starlight. Captain Croly's large room in the forward part of the vessel was the popular resort, and we spent evening after evening there, singing and conversing. On a Saturday evening the captain reminded us that the sailors' sentiment considered appropriate to that time, was "Sweethearts and Wives." He proposed that every one should tell a love story; "not a second-hand one," he stipulated, "but a little bit of personal experience. I'll start first, and when I 'heave to,' Nichols must have his sails set ready to follow. I daresay he won't be at any loss, and if he is, I can tell you some famous stories about him, for I used to know him on Cape Cod, when we were both young chaps." He then gave a laughable account of his own doings, closing with a story of a fair lady passenger, and five years of waiting before she became his wife. The threat had so good an effect on Captain Nichols that he portrayed some interesting experiences. Of course the young ladies had nothing to say on such a subject, but they listened and applauded, or made adverse criticisms. When Arthur's turn came he told a story of true love of a most romantic nature, which, at its climax, brought the gentlemen on their feet from sofas and easy chairs, and finding by the *denouement* that "all was right," they surrounded him with shouts of congratulations on the hopes before him. A beautiful face was exhibited in the back cover of his watch which excited general admiration, and the captain, giving him a resounding slap on the shoulder, declared that there wasn't a better story than that in the whole range of fiction. As Mr. Hamilton was unable to tell such a tale he declined to enter the lists.

The next evening we were assembled as usual in the same place, but the captain did not favor us with his company, being engaged in navigating the steamer up the river, for we had entered the Yang-tse-kiang, and anchored at ten o'clock to wait for daylight. In the morning the

"Aphrodite" started again, but soon ran aground, and there we were, stuck fast in the mud, with the sweet prospect of remaining within twelve miles of Shanghai until the next morning. Our patience was not so tried, though, for after tiffin a steam-tug was discovered, and Arthur, Amy, and I took passage in her for the city. What became of the other passengers I really did not inquire. They must have found some way of transportation, and I am glad it was not on that same steam-tug, for my spirits were like a glass of soda that bright October afternoon as we went up the Yang-tse-kiang, and I could not refrain from executing a kind of sailor's hornpipe on the little deck, knowing there were no eyes to observe me save those of my cousins, or perhaps of far-off Chinamen on the low, green banks.

On approaching the city the attention is first attracted by the "Concession," as the quarter allotted to foreign residents is called. A wide street, the "Bund," runs along the quay, and

Shanghai Hack. — Page 265.

handsome houses surrounded by trees are built upon it. Public buildings and church spires appear among the dark, glossy foliage peculiar to the tropics, and give to the "Concession" the appearance of being the most important part of Shanghai, as it certainly is the cleanest. The Chinese city is a large one, not remarkable for anything, cleanliness included, after one has seen Canton, we were told, and we never went within its walls. Hearing Canton called "comparatively clean" rather quenched my ardor respecting the native cities of this empire. As we walked along the "Bund," inquiring the way to Mr. Ingraham's dwelling, we saw a public conveyance that took my fancy more than any coupé ever did. It was a wheelbarrow with a partition in the middle of it, making seats for two passengers, who are trundled over the smooth ground for the payment of a few cents, and seem to enjoy themselves. Presently one came along with a woman on one side of the partition, and a pig on the other, balancing her. How I yearned for a ride! Not with a pig for balance, but if Amy only *would*— and of course, I knew she wouldn't, even if Arthur had not suggested that Mrs. Ingraham would think she had some strange American visitors if she saw them advancing to her home in a wheelbarrow.

In the course of time we came to a large house situated in a courtyard, and some stranger told us it was the residence of Mr. Ingraham. A lovely lady greeted us as eagerly expected friends, and we had cause to be satisfied with our welcome. What a delightful evening that was! In a most homelike parlor, where a blazing coal fire gave us a curious sensation of having been suddenly transported to our New England home after our tropical wanderings, we made the acquaintance of several pleasant people who had been asked to meet us, and I enjoyed above all things talking to our hostess and her brothers about their absent sister, giving them little episodes of her school life; while they drank in every word, telling me that seeing one who had been thus associated with her seemed to bring her near to them.

We devoted the next forenoon to Shanghai missions, and first drove out of town to visit a girls' boarding-school, an attractive house, where we were pleased with the airy dormitories and sunny school-rooms, the contented faces of the pupils, and the kind ones of their teachers; and after a tour of inspection, and a rest upon an upper balcony to see through climbing vines a view of green rice fields, and a level, dusty highway, they took us into a neat little chapel, and there the assembled girls sang some Sunday-school hymns before we went away. One of the missionary ladies came for us a day or two after to call on two families of Christian Chinese. They were humble people; yet from their manners we thought they had studied the Apostle Paul's directions for the truest kind of courtesy, and that they considered cleanliness to be next to godliness. However poverty may appear in a heathen home, you are sure to see the altar decorated with gilt paper and gaudy flowers, and the household deities standing there to be worshipped, but in these dwellings such things did not appear. The head of one family is a very intelligent young man who is studying for the ministry, and I wish you could have seen how glad he looked when he spoke of his future work among his countrymen. If the emperor had offered him some important office it would have seemed insignificant to him, according to what he said to us, compared with the high honor of being "put in trust with the Gospel." As we shook hands with him before leaving the house we told him we would pray that he might be faithful, and his work blessed.

It would be difficult to believe that there are anywhere more uninteresting drives than those around Shanghai. The country is a dead level, the roads are generally shadeless, and the sun-scorched fields on each side are decorated with large mounds, the graves of deceased Mongolians.

Yet on a cool autumn afternoon, to drive toward the setting sun in a high buggy with the top thrown back, drawn by two steeds that seem to tread on air, is not at all disagreeable, particularly with an entertaining companion. This was Amy's experience, while Arthur and I were part of a cheerful company in a beach wagon, and enjoyed ourselves extremely. To return after dark and scramble to get ready for an eight o'clock dinner, at which there are half a dozen guests, and perhaps a whole dozen courses, is the next thing after our drives; and these long dinners are not tiresome if one has even a moderately interesting person for an escort to the table, and neighbor during the next two hours, but it sometimes happens otherwise in my case. There are varieties in the human species, my friend, and I have sat through dinners beside such dismal specimens of mankind, that I could have eaten dry crackers and smoked herrings under the shadow of a tombstone with better appetite and spirits than were mine on those occasions.

The greatest event of our short visit in Shanghai was an excursion up the river to see an ancient pagoda. We went in two "house-boats" that have little cabins like yachts, into which five people could squeeze in case of rain coming on; but as the afternoon was perfect, we occupied the few square feet of deck room in the bows. Amy and Mrs. Ingraham were the only ladies on the leading boat, and one lady, with myself, composed the feminine portion of the company on the other, and all our companions were of the kind that know how to be entertaining; there was not one of them of the character I have alluded to above. (And I did not refer to any people in Shanghai more than in other places, when I made such a disparaging comment on partners at the dinner-table.) After an hour's sail our boats suddenly turned into a little creek, and we landed to walk through the cotton fields to the tall pagoda standing between us and the sunset, and throwing the shadow of its seven stories across our path. A massive structure it is, and bears the marks of age, yet it seems quite likely to stand erect through many more autumnal typhoons. I hope this aged monument of heathenism will be furnished with new flights of stairs for the benefit of curious travellers who shall come after us, that no civilized necks may be sacrificed. As for Chinamen, I think they are wary enough to keep out of it.

After a toilsome climb, our party came out upon a narrow platform that surrounds the seventh story, and the three voyagers from the "Lyra," with eyes long used to the oppressive mountain walls of Hong Kong, drew freer breath as we looked far, far away over that level land; and Amy said she realized there for the first time the *vastness* of China. Dimly blue on the horizon appeared three mountains of nearly the same size, and beside these distant promontories there was nothing in any quarter to break the monotony of that wide plain. Our descent was difficult and dangerous, and I wanted to turn myself around and go down backward, as one does on a ladder; but the others went down face foremost, so I did not choose to adopt crab fashions. There is a Buddhist temple near the pagoda, and we wandered into it. Three great idols stand therein, and many more of a smaller size, I suppose they must be; but I noticed only those three forms, which looked gigantic in the dusk. This excursion of ours claimed to be a picnic, and the picnic part of it consisted in our having supper as we floated down to Shanghai, our boats fastened together for convenience in passing the refreshments, and borne along by the current. It was lovely in that soft evening light to glide down the river, feasting on sandwiches, with ice-cream and white grapes! There were servants to wait on us, and the refinements of life to the extent of delicate china, damask napkins, silver spoons, and glass finger-bowls had been provided. Alas for this degraded taste of mine, which makes me most thoroughly enjoy picnics where you take pies and doughnuts with your fingers from a newspaper in your lap! But I do affirm that too much gentility has at times affected my appetite more than grief or care ever did, though you would not have thought it on this evening could you have seen me dispatch ice-cream. Happily none of us eat enough to prevent a vocal concert after supper, and we sang until the reflection of the city lights in the water eclipsed that of the stars. This was our last evening with the delightful Shanghai friends. On the following morning we parted regretfully from them, as the "Aphrodite" started for Amoy. This passage was quite unlike our former one. No social hilarity could prevail, for there was an extremely aristocratic party on board, who created an atmosphere of their own, and it was a very frigid one, causing our jovial Captain Croly to assume the character of a sedate, dignified commander, which was a lamentable change, in our estimation. Captain Nichols was again one of our fellow passengers, and he also was much subdued; yet when the "high caste" people all happened to be below, and our party, with two agreeable missionaries from Siam, had temporary possession of the deck, his spirits were in a measure revived. There was an interesting little girl belonging to the awe-inspiring party, who had not enough exclusiveness in her own possession to hinder her from making my acquaintance before we were fairly out of the yellow river, "Yang-tse-kiang," and she stayed with us a great deal of the time before and after stopping at Amoy. I always find real pleasure in the companionship of a child so intelligent and ladylike as this little May, and she would read poetry to me with wonderful expression, or sit quietly beside me while I taught her some fancy knitting-work.

Amy and I had an inferior state-room on this downward passage, and its upper berth was so near a wooden beam that I used to give my head a violent knock against it whenever I sat up, for I never could remember it was there until a collision had taken place, and sometimes I thought there must have been dents made on my skull.

Two days of vicissitudes and Amoy! "Not a nice place to look at, but far worse to smell," some one in Shanghai said of it in my hearing, and I agreed with the first part of his remark before we left the steamer; of the truth in the other clause we had yet to judge. A Chinese city at the foot of a range of barren hills was on one side of the harbor, and on the other a little island where foreign residents live, and to that place we went late in the afternoon to take tea at a missionary home.

Our path from the boat-landing gave us wild views of sea and rocks; green vines, and grass, and flower-gardens around the scattered houses there were indeed, but the general aspect of the place was sterile, lonely, and great boulders of most curious shapes seemed to me, as we passed them in the twilight, like enchanted monsters, petrified dragons and griffins, set there to guard this weird island. My unearthly fancies were quite dispelled as we crossed the threshold of a pleasant house, and were led into brightly-lighted rooms with words of hearty welcome. It was like turning from some German hobgoblin tale to a familiar picture of New England life, for these dear people had preserved the flavor of their own and our native land, and it was not only the old-fashioned pumpkin pie they gave us for supper that made us conscious of it. We spent a charming evening, and when, after praying and singing, we rose to take leave, some of the missionaries volunteered to show us the city of Amoy the next morning; or rather, the wonderful rocks upon the hills behind it, for the city itself, they assured us, was "nothing at all after Canton, and only remarkable for dirt." We returned to the steamer in a funny little sampan — an open one, with a cane seat in the middle just large enough for three people, and the boatman, standing behind us, used his single oar with such vigor that we sped over the dark waves and reached the "Aphrodite" almost too quickly.

Our experience of Amoy's uncleanliness began with the sedan chairs hired for our tour among the hills. If I did any justice to them by a description, I might find some improper words in this part of my letter when I came to read it over, therefore I refrain; but there were tatters, also cobwebs, and one could not help thinking that smallpox might be lurking in the grimy folds of the curtains. The streets, of course, were very narrow and crooked, and I believe I could have counted from twenty to thirty different odors, each worse than the last, as we were borne around sharp corners, up straggling lanes, where black pigs and yellow children appeared quite as blissful as if they had had pure oxygen to breathe. The people of Amoy do a great deal of cooking out in the streets, frying in rancid oil many of their delicacies, and the foreign barbarian who is unable to appreciate these savory dishes, goes on his way with elevated nose and face of extreme disgust. It makes me laugh to see the expressions of our little company, at least of those whose noses were not protected by handkerchiefs. I would not cover mine, for I was no less determined to see all there was to see, than to smell all there was to smell, and Arthur said I inhaled the breezes as if they came from a garden of jessamines!

Out at last upon the hills we came in the glare of noonday, and left our chairs to climb among the rocks that seem to have been tossed about there during a warfare of giants. One boulder of eighty tons' weight is so nicely balanced upon a rocky ledge that they say a strong wind can lift it, and under one end of it is a little cottage that would be crushed like an eggshell if it ever happened to tip over too far in that direction. We ran down a steep path to see who lived there, and found a family who gazed at us with astonishment. The old grandmother was spokeswoman, and in answer to an inquiry in Chinese if she were not afraid to live so near the rock, said, "No indeed, it was good luck, good Fung Shuey." Now, "Fung Shuey" is neither beast, man, nor spirit, but an influence, if I understand what one of the gentlemen told me; the good influence comes from the south, the bad from the north; therefore any high object, whether rock, hill or pagoda, that interposes between a dwelling and the north, has a beneficent effect on those who live in it, and this is why the old woman takes comfort in her balancing rock.

Some of the younger people gathered about us with observant eyes, and the grandame's fancy was gratified by the Hamburg edging on my cambric dress, which she fingered curiously, and then, taking a general survey of us, she exclaimed, "They are all *beautiful!*" That we might not feel too much flattered, but learn what estimate to place upon Chinese compliments, one of the ladies told us that a member of the mission had been followed by the remark, "How beautiful she is — just like the goddess of Mercy!" which sounds well, unless you remember that great ears, and a face painted with scarlet and gilt are always the distinguishing attractions of that honored lady.

There were temples perched upon the rocks, and some natural ones were formed by the rocks themselves, their great granite walls leaning toward one another, making cool, shadowy retreats, where, after the stony pathway, we rested our feet upon a soft green turf, and our eyes from the surrounding glare. In such a place I felt the deep, sweet meaning of these words applied to our Saviour, "The shadow of a great rock in a weary land." That land was indeed a "weary" one, you would have thought, looking over the arid hills with their masses of stone to the wretched city, where thousands of precious souls are as sheep having no Shepherd, and I asked one of the Christian workers at my side, who had left a pleasant American home to seek those souls for her Master's sake, if the shadow in which we were resting reminded her of that verse in Isaiah.

"Often," she replied, leaning her head restfully upon the solid granite behind us; "and His shadow has been as real and comforting to me in the dusty lanes of yonder city, where I have been seeking to do His will, as this great shadow is to us now, as we sit here upon the moss, with ferns springing up around us. There are 'sermons in stones,' surely, and these always preach to me when I come out here. When we stand on this wide platform of rock," she added with a smile, as we left our resting-place and walked out upon it, "is it not appropriate to sing,

> 'How firm a foundation, ye saints of the Lord,
> Is laid for your faith in His excellent Word!'

And many precious thoughts come as doves to their windows. 'The foundation of God standeth sure,' and 'Who is a rock save our God?' Come now, and peep into that cave just before us," said she, taking my hand. I stooped to look in, and there was barely light enough to see a frightful idol standing as the presiding deity, over whom spiders had irreverently spun their webs. "It looks ancient enough to have been standing there for generations, Miss Leigh," I said, and she replied:

"Let me quote another Bible verse for a motto upon this cave and its grim inhabitant: 'And the idols shall He utterly abolish, and they shall go into the holes of the rocks, and into the caves of the earth, for fear of the Lord, and for the glory of His majesty, when he ariseth to shake terribly the earth.' This old idol seems to me to foreshadow the fulfilment of that prophecy."

We entered a temple, where there was a row of small images on each side of the room, and one large one above a central altar. I sat down on a praying-stool before the principal idol, and taking a survey of them all, and also of an elderly priest who was in charge, my astonishment gave vent to itself in words. "Is it possible," said I to one of the missionaries, "that this sensible-looking old man actually worships these painted wooden things, and believes they are gods?" "I will ask him," was the reply; and after a short conversation in Chinese, the gentleman turned to me. "This is what he tells me: 'Oh, they may be gods and they may not be. Who can tell? But the priests must live—the people must have *something* to worship; and after all, I suppose it amounts to about the same thing as you Christians worshipping your God.'"

At that I turned around on my praying-stool, and with head bent on my hands I scrutinized the tiled floor and meditated. "Does it indeed amount to the same thing?" I asked myself. "Perhaps so, if we are only Christians in name, and perform the act of worship with a heart far from God; but if the Father has reconciled us to Himself through the death of His Son, and raised us up to a new life in Jesus, how immeasurable the distance between us and these benighted souls, and thanks be to Him forever for His undeserved mercy! As Faith says, we must do all we can to help them find our light, and leave them in God's hands."

The old priest begged us not to leave the hills before we had seen the "Tiger's Mouth," a cave which bears a resemblance to the open jaws of that animal. We could have a fine outlook upon the country from this cave, he said, and so we did, if any view of such a dreary country could be called fine, and then we descended the rocky slopes to take our sedan chairs again, and once more encountered the offences of Amoy. This time my handkerchief did me good service, for I no longer had any heart to enjoy the novelty and variety of the odors.

We crossed the harbor, and dined with one of the mission families in a pretty little cottage built near the sea-ward point of the island, where the cooling breeze, and the murmur of the waves coming in through open doors and windows, made me so drowsy after our morning's pilgrimage that I should have preferred a long siesta to my dinner.

Our steamer sailed for Hong Kong that afternoon, and the two following days of the voyage passed as the others had in the pleasant company of little May, and the young lady from Siam with her venerable father. It was late in the night when we entered Ly-Moon Pass, and all the harbor seemed asleep, but the piercing whistle of the "Aphrodite" announced her arrival, and boats came slowly up to take the passengers ashore. We went in a sampan to the "Lyra," whose gangway and cabin were illuminated, and her officers ready with their glad welcomes for us.

This fortnight has been one of rare experiences, which will long be kept among our treasures of memory, and as we like to have all our good things in common with you, dear friend, I hope, as I close my letter, that it may help you to share both the pleasure and the profit with us.

CHAPTER XI.

MACAO, AND RETURN TO HONG KONG.

AMY'S STORY.

"*Royal Hotel,*" *Macao, Nov. 5th, 18—.*

IN a great, barn-like room of this ambitiously-named house I am whiling away the hours of a rainy day, my friend, by writing to you. Marion and I are spending a few days in the Portuguese town which is chiefly associated in the public mind with the poet Camoens, who, for a satire upon the Viceroy of Goa, was banished from his home, and died here in exile. (Marion, looking over my shoulder, makes an objection: " You seem to take it for granted that Gussie is not a well informed young woman.

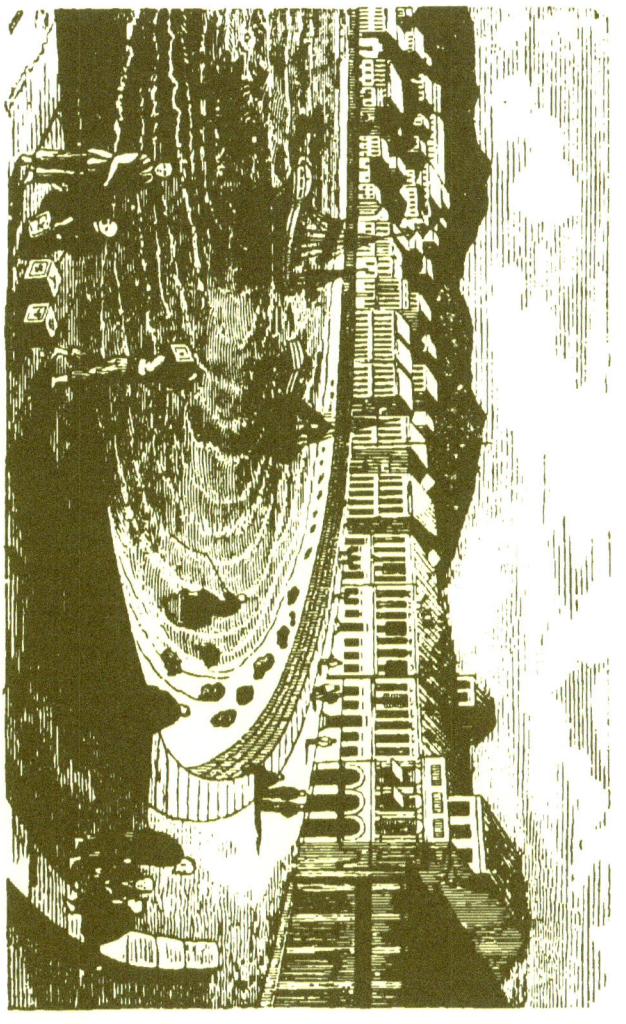

Macao.— Page 286.

Do you imagine she never heard of the man and his stupid Lusiad?" "Not at all," I reply. "I merely wanted to help her realize just where we are, and to fix the associations upon her mind.")

Mr. Dowling, who might be termed our "fairy godfather," transported us hither, and invited Mr. Duncan to be one of the party. The latter, in his joy at escaping from the ship for a season, left his sedateness behind, and became like a schoolboy off for a holiday, and during our three hours' voyage from Hong Kong in the steamer "White Cloud," we were all extremely merry.

Macao is built upon the sloping hillsides around a crescent-shaped bay. Its row of white and cream-colored houses on the curving Praya contrasts effectively with the deep blue of the waters that break against its granite sea-wall, and European travellers say it reminds them of some Italian town on the Mediterranean. The "Royal Hotel" stands upon the Praya, and from its front balcony we have the most stirring view afforded by this quiet town, from which the tide of commerce has been ebbing for many years, leaving it now a pretty watering-place, whither people from Hong Kong and Canton resort for rest, and the refreshment of its ocean breezes. In the evenings we look out on a more peaceful scene, as moonlight falls softly upon the sails of junks and sampans in the harbor, and transforms a white-plastered fort, gleaming among the heavy foliage, at one end of the crescent, into the likeness of a marble palace.

On our way here from the steamer, through the hilly streets, I saw from my sedan two women with a pole resting on their shoulders, and a trunk suspended from it. "Mr. Dowling!" I cried, in dismay, "do women carry the baggage in Macao?" Then I saw my own initials on the trunk, which was poor consolation, but I was glad there were no heavy things in it for the sake of those bare-footed porters toiling up the hills. Our chair-coolies were ordered to wait outside the hotel while we went to our rooms and rested; then we resumed our seats, and explored the outskirts of the town by the light of a setting sun.

The road led us to the summit of steep crags, where there was a wide view sea-ward, and far below among the rocks the waves broke in showers of spray. The rest of the way was less attractive, and through the heart of the town we came back to our hotel in time for a late dinner. There was not a crowd of guests sojourning there, we knew, yet I had not expected to see only a party of young men at the table beside ourselves and the host. One of them was a French count, and their conversation was in French, — decidedly frivolous, Marion and I considered it; and even with our slight knowledge of the language, it was evident that remarks were being made upon the "Americaines." That was rather trying to our composure, and I thought it fortunate that neither Mr. Dowling nor Mr. Duncan understood French, for the former would have been seriously annoyed at having his charges subjected to such impertinence, and I am sure Mr. Duncan would have been incensed. During the progress of these observations and of the courses, our host, Senor de Graça, became uneasy, and in a low tone inquired of Mr. Duncan if the young ladies spoke French. His answer was, "I believe not," but he did not add that we could understand it tolerably; it was quite likely that he was not aware of the fact, and De Graça continued his dinner with an air of relief.

We adjourned to the balcony, and the moonlight made Marion restless to go up to the cliffs we had passed before dinner, so our dear old guardian told Mr. Duncan that he might escort us there. As for himself, that would be too much of a scramble, after the events of the day. It was a scramble, certainly, for after mounting the hill to the sharp edge of the cliff, we went down over the rocks to the shore, Mr. Duncan helping us, one at a time,—not without peril to our necks. Once down there we did not repent of our rashness, for the waves came curling softly in, almost to our feet, and the sea shone in the light of a great golden moon, and we sat still in the shadow of a crag, quieted by a sense of the beauty before us.

Suddenly, with an English accent, these words broke the silence: "Yes, I think I know all about them. They must be the girls I heard of in Hong Kong who came to China on their brother's ship, that big one moored over on the Kow-Loon side, you know. He's one of the pious kind, they say; preaches to his men on Sundays, and goes to the hospital to talk to the sick sailors. A religious sea-captain! He must be a queer prig." "A natural curiosity, I should say," said another voice. (The talkers were a little higher up than we, and our crag screened us completely.) "Mais les demoiselles," said a third person, "ne pensez vous—" "As for the girls themselves," interupted the first speaker; but the expression of his opinion was cut short by Mr. Duncan, who rose hastily and pitched a great stone into the sea, thereby startling the intruders into silence. Then he said distinctly, "I think it is time for us to return." The strangers had a chance to retreat, of which they were not slow to take advantage, and a little gurgle of laughter from Marion followed them. I tried to keep her from such an outbreak, though I felt inclined to join in it, and she declared I half strangled her. Our faithful friend was more provoked than amused at this little episode, and a remark about "those impertinent fellows" came from under his moustache as he gave us a helping hand to climb up to the road.

The day's adventures ended with an experience of rats in our room, a great, bare place, where the scanty furniture hides away in the shadows, and over the uncarpeted floor an army of rats, we thought from the sounds, took lively exercise in the darkness. If there were only two or three they must have been monstrous ones, and they raced about as a herd of cattle might scour a prairie, while we actually quaked in our high bed. I lighted a candle at last, thinking it would be worse to have our foes attack us unseen, and as I did so a large rat disappeared through a hole in the bottom of the door. Then I stuffed a brown veil into the hole, foolishly supposing it would prevent the return of the rodent, and went peacefully to sleep, for his companions were less formidable. In the morning the hole was open — the veil gone! Mr. Duncan handed it to me when we met at breakfast, saying he found it on the floor of the hall. *We* knew how it came there, but refrained from any explanation.

With a pleasant old Portuguese guide named De Silva, we made an early start to find the curiosities of Macao, and he led us first to the Catholic Cathedral; then to see a grand ruin, that of St. Paul's Church, whose façade is standing, with a portion of its side and back walls; but where worshippers once knelt on the marble floor within, a little grove has grown up since fire made a ruin of the building, and the leafy branches bend over graves, for it is now used as a cemetery. A very long, wide flight of steps leads up to the stone court-yard before the church, and from that point of view I first saw the noble façade, venerably gray, and so perfect as to give me no idea that the church was a ruin until I had innocently exclaimed, "What a remarkably beautiful shade of blue the curtains in those windows have!" and was informed by my amused companions that I was looking through the apertures at the sky beyond.

We visited the Barracoon, where the poor coolies are kept while waiting to be shipped to other lands; and the Protestant burying ground, a spot chiefly interesting to us because of the grave of Dr. Morrison, the first missionary to China. He rests from his labors, and surely his works do follow him.

There is no place in Macao where travellers go with more interest than to Camoens' Gardens, where shadiness and seclusion are suggestive of meditative poets, and irregular paths winding among the trees afford bright little glimpses of the sea. The exile's tomb is there, near a grotto in which he doubtless passed many a homesick hour, and as we turned away after reading its inscription, I noticed Marion's woe-begone face and her weary, dragging step. "Amy," she said in a despairing tone, "I suppose you feel just the way you ought to — in the spirit of the place, and all that?" "Camoens certainly does seem very real to me," said I, "and just now these words of Mrs. Browning were in my mind, naturally suggested by a thought of poor Catrina dying at home, while her heart was here in exile with her poet,—"

> "On the door you will not enter
> I have gazed too long — adieu !
> Hope withdraws her peradventure,
> Death is near me, and not you.
>   Come, O lover,
>   Close, and cover
> These poor eyes you called, I ween,
> 'Sweetest eyes were ever seen !'"

"Oh, dear me!" she rejoined dolefully, "why can't I get up some nice, suitable feelings? I don't care anything about the man and his Catrina — I'm too tired and sleepy for any more sights, and in future years I shall reproach myself for having stood here before his tomb with no more emotion than if it were a great hen-coop! However, it can't be helped now, and one comfort remains to me; there is Mr. Duncan not at all concerned about Camoens, I know, yet he does enjoy these rural walks, and I can't even do that, because those rampaging rats last night destroyed my slumber."

After this wail from our Marion we left the gardens, and proceeded through the city streets to see whatever De Silva chose to show us. Only one thing more I will mention, a peep into a gambling house, and at a table where stood a breathless group, watching some mysterious performances with small stones, or pieces of ivory; and when a gain for one and loss for another was decided there were exclamations from all, and some face among the crowd acquired a deeper shade of wretchedness, yet fixed its gaze upon the table as if attracted by a fatal spell.

After dinner and a nap, we took an open carriage and went to the summit of a hill at one extremity of the island to visit the church of "Our Lady of Sorrows." A rude wooden cross stands before its portals, and our guide told us that a sea captain, during a violent storm, vowed that if he were saved, the mainmast of his vessel should be transformed into a cross and placed in that spot, which was done when he reached the shore in safety. From the parapet surrounding the church there is a glorious view of all Macao, the sea, and the hills of the neighboring land; and we rested there for a long time, scarcely heeding that the afternoon was slipping away, and De Silva longing to drag us away for fresh sights. We should have returned to Hong Kong to-day but for this drenching rain and Mr. Dowling's rheumatic liabilities. I do not object to this delay as I should were we not getting used to the rats at night, yet our resources in this hotel are limited to a jingling piano and a musty backgammon board. Marion and Mr.

Dowling are using the latter now, and I ought to go and relieve her, for more than one hour of that game would be severe discipline for her. The count and his party have betaken themselves to other scenes. They behaved very well at table after the first evening, and hardly glanced at us. So no more from Macao, I will continue after we are in our floating home again.

Hong Kong Harbor, Nov. 16th.

After this letter there will be no more dated in like manner, for at last the welcome order has come for the "Lyra" to proceed to Manila, there to be loaded with sugar, as hemp refuses to fall after all this waiting, which has been so much more profitable to *us* than to the vessel's owners. It has caused us some impatient feelings in the intervals between our various excursions, for Hong Kong has not been wholly delightful; yet now, as the time approaches when the "Lyra's tall masts will cease to be one of the familiar objects in this harbor, and the scenes and friends who have known us here shall know us no more, we find that many pleasant things day by day incline us to linger. We have told you nothing of the typhoon that agitated these waters a few weeks ago, and fully satisfied our curiosity respecting the storms which are the greatest dread of navigators in eastern seas. I have seen some elderly skippers shudder when Marion or myself thoughtlessly expressed a wish that we might "see a real typhoon," and if it could be so terrible in a sheltered harbor, what must such a tempest be to those exposed upon the open ocean! For several days previous to the typhoon the forces of nature seemed to be gathering for an outbreak. A strangely wild sky, sudden gusts of wind, and dark waves crested with white, instead of the usually tranquil waters of the harbor, kept us on the watch for something out of the usual course of things. The "Aphrodite" was then in port, and we were invited one evening to dine on board of that steamer to meet Captain Croly's wife and a few city guests, but waves and wind were so threatening that to go in our open boat was out of the question. The captain hailed a sampan, and we were about to embark in it when its owner informed us that he feared "one welly bad typhoon come — all the sampans go in safe place and stay all nightee;" therefore, as we saw no way of returning from the "Aphrodite," we gave up our anticipated pleasure, and sat on deck in the darkness listening to the increasing gale. "It is a typhoon, and no mistake," were the first words I heard in the morning, and with the dashing water and motion of the vessel we could have easily imagined ourselves at sea. The wind shrieked and whistled through the rigging, the rain poured down, and the "Lyra's" girls wrapped themselves in waterproofs and sat on the upper steps of the companion way, watching the wild scene, and enjoying it in a way that was almost wicked, I thought afterwards, when we heard that over one hundred Chinese were drowned that day in the harbor. Anchored so far from the city as our ship was, and with only a few near neighbors, there was no real danger for her, although she dragged her anchor, and the captain and mate appeared somewhat concerned about what she might do if the typhoon increased, and while we inconsiderate young things were rejoicing in this strife of the elements, there was great suffering and loss of life at the city quays. From houses on the Praya the inhabitants could see sampans tossed up against the stone wall, and Chinamen struggling in the waves, while great blocks of granite were dislodged from the solid masonry, and it was difficult to render any aid, one of the merchants told us, even to those who were perishing before their eyes.

When days went on again under bright blue skies, with a suggestion of autumnal coolness in the air, and the recent typhoon had nearly ceased to be the prevailing topic of social converse, our vessel was honored by a call that was far beyond common events, and has led since then to some of the greatest pleasures we have known in Hong Kong. The callers were two English ladies, which fact made their coming all the more remarkable, as there was not even the attraction of a common country to draw them all the way across to "Kow Loon side," to visit strangers on an American ship, and the only reason for their appearance was that an acquaintance of theirs spoke of us as people who would appreciate and enjoy the hospitalities of their beautiful home. "Who is my neighbor?" is a question that seems to be asked very often in this colony. "What are these people to me? Why should I have anything to do with them? They are not on the same level in society with myself," — is a free translation of the question. But these new friends of ours, Mrs. Carleton and her sister Miss Barrett, would say, " Our neighbors are all whom we can make happier by our society, or help in any way." Accordingly, it was upon their general principles that they invited us to tiffin and croquet; but it was not formally that the invitation was passed — they were as gushing, Marion declared, as if we had just come from their friends in Great Britian. After this prelude, you may imagine us setting out on an appointed day to find Mrs. Carleton's house, and our coolies bore us up through almost perpendicular streets to a road which is the highest in town, on the very edge of the mountain. There we travelled up and down for a long time, uncertain as to the place of our destination, and this afforded us a glimpse of a deep gorge in the hills, through which a stream, crossing our way, ran under a pretty stone bridge into a grove of pines below, and in the opening, at the lower end of the gorge, was framed a lovely little landscape — a bit of the harbor with the hills beyond, and a white church-spire in the foreground.

At last the house we sought was found: a one-storied bungalow, perched on the highest spot of any house in the colony, and commanding a view that is bewildering in its variety and beauty. The ladies were sitting on the front verandah with their work, and we rested there until the announcement of tiffin, a meal that is most pleasant for conversation, as it is apt to be unsubstantial, and may be regarded rather as a pastime than an affair of moment, particularly when a few of our sex gather around the board to sip delicious tea and peel bananas, after disposing of a first course of cold chicken and its accompaniments.

Arthur and a few other gentlemen joined the feminine party upon the verandah before the afternoon was far advanced, and the servants brought out little tables, and handed around that beverage with which all who live in this land are wont to refresh themselves so frequently that you might suppose the vital principle to be contained in every cup of tea.

An adjournment to the croquet ground was proposed, and upon a level, velvety platform, cut out of the steep mountain side, we played until the rosy flush of sunset on the hills and clouds had faded into a graver tint, and a new moon appeared over the sharply defined edge of the Peak behind us. Then we took leave of our hostesses and their other guests, having first accepted invitations to two croquet parties, one at the barracks, and one at the residence of a merchant in the city.

Croquet assemblies, sometimes ending with dinner parties, became the order of our days and evenings for a while, and when we were beginning to be tired of them new diversions succeeded. "We take tea on the 'Great Northern' to-night," announced our captain one day at the dinner table. "Who and what is the 'Great Northern?'" was our natural inquiry. "The steamer that came out from England to lay the telegraphic cable between Hong Kong and Shanghai; and you will have an opportunity of laying in a store of solid information, my children," said he. Assuredly, it was not for lack of opportunity if we did not lay in such a store that evening, for the captain of this steamer took us to the telegraphic apartment, where there was an electrician ready to explain everything to us; then we were shown the machines for laying the cable, and Marion's head, she told me, was in a whirl from inability to comprehend half we had seen and heard. Perhaps other heads in the party were in the same condition. At tea we made a few acquaintances; the one we liked best was an English lady with so unusual a name that I will not undertake to spell it for you. She was very friendly, and asked us to come the next night to her house, where a choral society would meet for a weekly rehearsal, and the idea of hearing any real music again after so long a deprivation sent us home with hearts bounding gaily, like our boat, as it bore us over the waves.

In the clear moonlight of a November evening three perplexed Americans might have been seen in sedan chairs, hunting the city streets for a house of which the owner's name, even, was a matter of doubt to them. To our no less perplexed coolies we gave a name that sounded as much like the right one as it could without being that, and after going back and forth, and up and down, we began to think that dinner and music were not for us that evening, when a stream of gas-light crossed our way from an open hall door, and there stood our friend in her floating white robes. She was looking out to discover the cause of the commotion in her quiet street, for when six bearers are uncertain where to carry their passengers, they discuss and argue the question so clamorously that you might suppose a serious quarrel was going on. That dinner had been delayed for us, I should think was quite probable, and those who at last took their places around a board brilliant with silver, glass, and flowers were "twelve piecee man," as a Chinese waiter would say, which includes the ladies.

Selections from Mendelssohn's "Four Part

Songs" formed the evening's programme. I had a chorus book, and joined occasionally in those joyous melodies which carry the thoughts away to green fields and forests. My "other half," Marion, kept herself in a secluded corner behind the singers, and was so earnestly engaged in conversation with a stout British officer, who stood beside her in the shadow of a window curtain, that I wondered more than once or twice what their argument could be. It concerned the first question in the Westminster Catechism, "What is the chief end of man?" she told us as we were walking down to the boat. "Didn't he consider that rather a novel subject to discuss at a party?" we asked her. "Perhaps so, but I did not force it upon him at all," Marion said. "We fell into the argument quite unexpectedly and naturally, and he pursued it with so much interest that I did not take any pains to change the subject." "Well, little girl," said Arthur, encouragingly, "I don't believe he got any too much of it, or he would not have responded so heartily afterward when I invited him to call on us. You will have a chance to ask him the second question if you wish to.

Our next move was a picnic to Douglas Castle; a nautical picnic, in one sense (although the company went by land to the other side of the island), for it consisted exclusively of seafaring people — plenty of captains, the wives of two, and the daughter of one of them, besides a delegation from the "Lyra;" and with heavy provision baskets we went to that mysterious castle by the sea. I call it mysterious because everything about it *is* a mystery to me. If it was built for a home (though its great rooms are so unhomelike) why is it deserted now, save by one or two servants or keepers? Silence reigns there, except on days when pleasure parties like ours awaken its echoes, and explore its lofty halls and chambers. It is reported that a newly married pair, not caring to take a long wedding tour, yet desiring to spend a part of their honeymoon away from the noisy city, came to Douglas

Castle for that purpose, but two or three days of its ghostly silence and damp, chilly atmosphere sufficed, and the bride groom declared when they came back to everyday life that it was too lonely to be endured any longer. None of the apartments were cheerful enough for our merry dinner party, and a long table was spread in a very draughty verandah, where the sea wind, which could not spoil our cold viands, sharpened the appetites and brightened the wits of all. Hong Kong influences had contaminated every one of us to some degree, as was proved by our beginning to gossip when hunger was partially appeased. Innocent gossip it was, and entirely good-natured. The subject thereof was a German bride, who had caused a pleasant excitement in the community by coming all the way from the Fatherland to meet her lover, the captain and owner of a pretty bark, which is one of our nearest neighbors. One morning it made such a gorgeous display of flags that the public were led to inquire what could be the news from Germany, but it was known before many hours that the Captain's wedding, not patriotism, was the excuse for his vessel's festive array. The German girl is said to be radiantly beautiful, and "Who has seen her?" was the question at our table. "I met her in the gardens on 'Band afternoon,'" said one. "I saw her through a spy-glass from my deck when she first went aboard the bark," confessed another, and he added that she was "a picture." "She is as pretty as she can be to stay in her skin," proclaimed old Captain Bird, and this peculiar testimony, given with authority, closed our discussion of the bride for that time, at least.

"You are all noisy enough up there," some one called from the road below, and in a moment young Mr. Weir, of the house of Gainsborough & Co., joined us on the verandah, asking if a land-lubber could be admitted to such a gathering of "salts." "I walked up the Peak this afternoon from the city," he said, "and coming down on this side, heard your voices before the castle was in sight, so I had to stop here to see what the fun was. And here is Miss Roslyn," continued Mr. Weir, "the very person I had made up my mind to see to-day, as I have an important request to make of her." To be short, my Gussie, he wanted me to present a prize, called "The Ladies' Purse," at the yearly Regatta, which was to occur in a few days. The time-honored custom that it should be presented by a young member of the single sisterhood brought difficulties this year, for there are few white damsels in Hong Kong, and two of them had rejected Mr. Weir's proposal, on the ground that they had performed the part before. As a last resort, therefore, he thought "Miss Roslyn" might do, and that young lady reluctantly consented to oblige him, if he would promise to write a short speech for her to commit to memory, and deliver when the successful oarsman should appear for his prize. He said he would do so, and we dispersed in small detachments. Some of us went up to the white turrets on the castle roof and watched the sun dip into the China sea, and when evening shades fell over us the rovers assembled, and our procession took up its line of march.

Regatta day came, and no sign of a speech from Mr. Weir; not even an opening sentence, — and how was I to know what sort of things Hong Kong ladies said on such occasions? He had promised to write it for me "word for word." "Vain indeed are the promises of man!" said Marion, but putting our three heads together we wrote a speech at last, and I committed it to memory. We went on board the "Australia," a great English steamer anchored by the racecourse, where the *élite* of the city came also to witness the performances, and dispose of a cold collation. The sight of about two hundred strangers made me feel smaller than Mrs. Tom Thumb, and I longed to shrink into an atom and hide in Arthur's pocket, for stares were never bestowed with more effrontery than they were upon me that afternoon, — and it was not my imagination, truly. There were a dozen good friends of ours among the crowd, and one or two of them managed to divert me so pleasantly that I forgot my nervous fears, and ceased my mental repetition of the speech. Suddenly I became aware that a small space was cleared around me, and the prominent figures in it were myself and a young man who had on a flannel boating-shirt, and he stood there looking embarrassed, yet expectant. It was a wonder that I did not forget what I had to say to him, but I launched out upon my speech, groping meantime in my pocket for the blue velvet purse, heavy with gold sovereigns. This I extricated, and held out to the youth, who seized it eagerly, and muttered a few words of gratitude. *I* was the grateful one to have the ordeal over, and all I wanted was to escape from the "Australia." Instead of that, the Chairman of the Regatta Committee handed me down to the saloon, and gave me the seat of honor at his right hand, a most uncoveted position; still, as my mind was relieved, I could do what politeness required of me in paying attention to the eatables, and listened with some amusement to the talk and toasting.

There will be now only a few days before our departure for Manila, and yesterday, our last Sunday here, we took leave of a place that is to me the dearest in Hong Kong — the quiet chapel, where so many times we have been taught and encouraged. Dr. Legge preached from this text: "The harvest truly is plenteous, but the laborers are few," and as we passed out under the stone arches to go down among the busy multitudes I seemed still to hear his closing appeal, "Will you not, my friends, each one of you, ask the Lord to send you out as a laborer into His great harvest-field, the world?" During the row home, though the sky was nearly covered with gray clouds, the eastern hills, brilliantly illuminated by the setting sun, made me think of Christians living in the light and joy of the Lord, unshadowed by the clouds of trouble, witnessing to all of that peace passing understanding which comes from the glory of His presence.

We were standing this afternoon on Mrs. Carleton's smooth green sward, engaged in a game of croquet, when some one said, "There goes the 'Great Republic,'" and I dropped my mallet to see the American mail steamer leave the harbor on her way to our native land. Six steamers have come and gone since we arrived in Hong Kong; each one bringing pleasant news from our absent friends, and bearing to them accounts of our happiness here! Goodness and mercy have followed us continually, and when we sail for other foreign shores there will be a song of praise in our hearts as we look back over these six months in China.

CHAPTER XII.

MANILA.

Manila, Dec. 28th, 18—.

WE have crossed the China Sea to the Philippine islands, and are enjoying a life of luxury in the tropics such as I have dreamed of on many a summer-day, never thinking to experience. At the house of a hospitable merchant in one of the surburban villages that lie around Manila, the "Lyra's" passengers are handsomely entertained, and our kind host and hostess meet all expressions of our gratitude with repeated assurances that our visit is a favor to them ; a halcyon state of things, as we were strangers of whom they had only heard through friends in Hong Kong during our long stay there!

I am writing out of turn, as last month's communication came from my hand, but Marion has so large a pile of mail matters weighing on her mind that I told her she must forego the pleasure of a letter to her Gussie, and attend to those which I could not undertake for her.

Will you believe we had more difficulty and danger in coming over here from Hong Kong than in rounding Cape Horn? It was even so, as I will explain, and to begin an account of our ten days' voyage, I must say that sea-sickness laid hold upon us before China was fairly out of sight; not severely in my case, for Marion found me in my berth, singing from a book that lay open before me. I asked her to join me, telling her I was keeping the malady at bay, but she was not in a tuneful frame, and preferred to have "a good, square fit of sickness," for which purpose she shut herself into the opposite state-room.

We regained our equilibrium in a day or two and resumed our methodical sea-life, to some extent, in sewing and reading aloud to each other. Homer's Iliad (Lord Derby's translation) was the work with which we beguiled a rather disagreeable passage across the China Sea, and for days the weather was rainy or cloudy, until there came a calm, fair Sunday, when on the horizon Luzon's blue mountains appeared. If we supposed that there was nothing before us but a speedy sail into Manila Bay, it was a mistake, indeed, for baffling winds and perplexing currents met the "Lyra," and drove her in a zigzag course among dangerous rocks and islands, and on the evening of November 29th, the captain resolved to anchor where the wooded "Corregidor," curving toward another island, formed a sheltered bay, and to wait there for morning. He was tired out, poor fellow, after a week of anxious navigation, and when the anchor was dropped he did not refuse dressing-gown and slippers, and an arm-chair in the cabin where I was reading "Dombey" aloud, while the rain pattered on the skylight. Suddenly our comfort was put to flight by Mr. Duncan bursting in upon us with bad news. "She's dragging, sir!" he cried, and Arthur, getting quickly into rubber coat and boots, found it too true. The anchor had not taken a firm hold on the sandy bottom, and there was danger, if the wind had risen, of the vessel's stranding on "Corregidor." To heave the anchor, and sail on in the foggy darkness would have been as much of a risk as to remain where we were; but daylight relieved our fears, showing that the anchor had been dragged only a short distance. Away we sailed under clearer skies, and congratulated ourselves upon the prospect of a speedy arrival in Manila. The track we had been making, as shown by Arthur's chart, was a labyrinth of zigzag lines, often recrossing the same spot three or four times, and at the end of four days of constant "tacking" it reached the point where it began.

The sun had gone down free from all clouds, save a few gold and purple specks that lingered in his track, and a half moon began to whiten the sails as Marion and I walked up and down on the house, arm in arm, talking cheerily of the past six months' events, and planning a distribution of presents among the friends at home. Arthur stood below on the deck, intently watching the forward sails. "We are all right now, are we not?" Marion called to him. "If this breeze holds until we pass the next island, 'Caballo,'"—but almost as he spoke the light wind died away, and a strong current bore us toward an island that rose up from the sea in a steep bluff. Now, near enough to hear the waves roll up on the beach and crickets singing among the trees, our hearts stood still, for we knew that our ship was in peril.

"Let go the anchor!" rang out the captain's voice, sharp and strained, as we had never heard it, and in one moment more there was a bumping, grating sound under us, and the great helpless ship had gone on the sands.

A commotion ensued; orders were shouted, and men rushed to and fro obeying them. We poor girls, bewildered, hardly knowing the extent of the trouble, but believing that shipwreck stared us in the face, went below to be out of the way and calm ourselves as best we could by considering the situation. Our ideas of the threatened shipwreck were vague, but we knew that a sudden gale of wind might easily drive the "Lyra" upon the beach, and our voyage thus be sadly ended.

"What will become of us if we have to go ashore?" Marion asked me. "There is a lighthouse there, and we should take refuge in it, I suppose, but it is well known that the Spaniards on these islands are not apt to be friendly to foreigners. However," I added, "we might as well be ready for what may come, and I can't go scrambling through woods and swamps with these thin shoes on;" so I put on thick boots, and advised Marion to do the same. "Don't talk of boots," she said, dolefully. "Only think of losing all the lovely things we bought in China!" "Oh! they will save them probably, even if the ship never gets off again; but our precious 'Lyra!' Think of leaving her to go to pieces here! No, *don't* think of it while there is hope. Let us go up on deck and see what they are doing to save her."

Some of the sailors had the small kedge anchor in one of the boats, with a rope attached to it, of which one end was around the capstan, and rowing off about a quarter of a mile, they dropped it into deep water, then the men on board the ship worked hard at the capstan, turning it round and round, singing meantime to help them pull hard together. All the familiar songs which used to make us merry on happy evenings sounded at this time to our ears like dirges over a lost ship. Eagerly we watched the rope on which so much depended, fearful that it could not bear the strain, and almost imperceptibly the ship moved backward toward the buried anchor. At last, when nearly midnight, Mr. Duncan gave a joyful shout, "There she swings!" and once more the "Lyra" was afloat. To raise a few sails and put a safe distance between ourselves and "Caballo" was the next action, and in the morning we looked back at its faint outlines with very thankful hearts for our deliverance.

One more day and night of slow sailing brought us into the wide, open harbor of Manila, where the few vessels at anchor seem very far apart, not neighborly as in Hong Kong; and flowing into it, the Pasig river bears down myriads of drifting plants from the great Lake Bay in the interior of the island. The city is built along the river banks, and there is nothing beautiful in its aspect, yet even to live there, we thought, would be better than to remain in the harbor with nothing at all to see. Several American gentlemen came off at once to call upon us.

One of them was Mr. Irvine, who told us that his wife had made preparations to receive us at their house in Santa Ana, and he hoped we would stay with them as long as the "Lyra" remained in port.

Through a gateway in the massive city wall we drove into Manila, where are gloomy Spanish houses, with few windows high above the street, and gray old churches in every stage of dilapidation. "This one," said Mr. Irvine as we drove past a ruin, "was shaken down in the earthquake of 1843, and the one you see at the end of the street suffered from the earthquake of 1852," and so on, until we thought we had come to a very unsettled part of the earth. There were enough whole churches, though, most of them ugly and weather-stained. Tagal (native Indian) women in gay costumes walked the streets, or stood about shop-doors in the public squares. One fashion of dress is closely followed by all. It consists of a skirt striped in the brightest colors, and a piece of cloth of another color fastened over it like a tightly-drawn overskirt; a loose jacket, and a handkerchief above that, with the ends crossed in front, complete the costume. The men all wear their shirts hanging airily outside their trousers, and look as if it were the chief business of life to keep cool and lounge on street corners, amusing themselves with fighting-cocks.

The Calzadas, a wide, shady avenue, leads from the dingy town into rural scenes, where on either hand stretch rice-fields of brilliant green, and thatched huts of the Indians are upon the roadside among tall bamboos, wide-spreading mango trees, and the great, glossy leaves of the plantain. There are the well-built and painted dwellings of the better class of Indians, or of the Mestizos, a race of people partly Tagal and partly European, many of whom are very wealthy, and in the midst of the luxuriant gardens are a few large houses occupied by foreign merchants. Into one of these we drove after coming to the suburban village of Santa Ana; *into* it, literally,

Tagal Women. — Page 328

for instead of a front door is an archway through which the carriage passes into a stone-paved hall, and we, alighting there, were led up a flight of stone steps to the second floor, always the dwelling place in Manila houses. At the head of them stood a lady to receive us, and never, I am sure, did two sea-faring girls find themselves welcomed into a more beautiful home.

From a wide hall that they call the "cayeda" open, spacious apartments on either hand, with polished floors and cane furniture, from any one of which we step into a tiled corridor where the sliding sashes are thrown back to admit the air and light. There are no glass panes in them, for in this region of earthquakes that article is generally dispensed with because of its frailty, and its place supplied by oyster-shells, ground and polished, and each fitted into its own socket. They are not transparent, and light is subdued by them as much as if they were of thick ground glass, which must be an objection in the rainy season when the casements often have to be closed.

Marion and I felt almost lost in the great room that was given to us, and were bewildered with so much space. In our adjoining dressing-room there were huge bowl-shaped tubs of stone or bronze, filled to the brim with water, and after surveying these with some amazement we wandered out into our own especial corridor, and were charmed to find that it overlooked the Pasig river, flowing down beyond the distant city, and a peculiar rustle made always by a breeze among banana leaves mingled pleasantly with the murmur of its swift current. "It is more like a fairy tale than anything has been yet," said Marion in rapture, leaning out to gaze far up the winding river. "We are like two princesses in the Alhambra, with our lofty walls and marble pavements, and we are going to have a great deal better time than any of those poor souls ever had."

Arthur was unable to share with us the elegancies of shore life ; his presence being required on the ship, for Mr. Duncan was not at all well, and a new comer occupied the position formerly held by Mr. Fordyce, who left us in Hong Kong. (Did I tell you in my last letter? He was sorry to leave, but had a chance to be mate in a homeward bound vessel.) Our captain gladly avails himself of an invitation to be with us whenever he can leave his duties, and makes morning calls in our corridor to read and talk over home letters, or he appears at dinner-time and meets the foreign element in the evening.

As we sit around the table, at the lower end of the "cayeda," enjoying fruit and coffee at our leisure, steps are heard upon the stone stairs, and we hurriedly adjourn to the parlor, there to receive our callers ; American, Scotch, and English, partners and clerks, elderly and young ; so many gentlemen that it brings my mind into a state of confusion to try to remember their names and attach them to their proper owners. Our host is most diligent at all times and seasons to impress upon us the fact that our visit here is causing a commotion among this part of society (I mean the bachelors), because the coming to this island of young ladies from the United States is an event of more rare occurrence than an earthquake, and perhaps only less so than the appearance of a comet. We are assured that the "Lyra's" arrival, and the kind of passengers she would bring, had been matters of speculation in Manila for months before that vessel left Hong Kong, and any one who came here from the latter port was called upon to contribute his knowledge of the subject for the public good. One report that came before us was that said lady passengers were "both thirty-five years old at least, and blue stockings of the severest description!" What could we have done or looked like to deserve that? On some evenings, when there are five or six callers at once, we do not have a chance for conversation with all, and so it was in the case of "the man who had great expectations," as Marion will call him. He sat at a little distance from us, conversing with Mr. Irvine, and would frequently survey us with an air of such — what shall I say? disapproval or disappointment — that we came separately to this conclusion: he had expected two extraordinary beings, and as his ideas were rapidly descending before the reality, was mentally exclaiming, "What a fall is here, my countrymen!" He has never made a second call. Those who pleased us the best on first acquaintance come here often, and we spend the evenings very informally when they are our visitors, often gathering around the piano for singing, or near the chess table, if Marion or myself have been challenged to a contest with the ivory men.

The days begin with a meeting of the family in the "cayeda" for "desayuno," or early breakfast, a light meal of toast, cold meat, guava jelly, etc., and then comes a drive into town while the morning breezes are refreshing. Not always into the city, really, unless there is shopping to be done; oftener the carriage is drawn up on a grassy common near the sea, where we look at the ships, and inhale the salt air, and after a pause go back to Santa Ana, glad to seek shelter in the cool house from heat that by ten o'clock is often intense on these December days.

From eleven to one, a sewing and reading circle with our hostess, then "breakfast," which corresponds with "tiffin" in China, and a long afternoon spent in our corridor with books or writing, until the monotone of the river among the rustling plantains assists an overpowering drowsiness, and a siesta must be indulged in.

As shadows lengthen we awake, and prepare for the pleasantest hour of the day — sunset, when every one goes out to drive, and in a barouche we roll toward the town again. If it is band night on the Lunetta, a lamp-lit park close to the water, the wide common is astir with countless barouches, and social intercourse goes on in Spanish and English. Dark-eyed ladies lean back on the carriage cushions, and wave their fans languidly as young cavaliers advance to pay their respects, and some of our friends, who are careering about on horse-back, ride up to bid us good evening, or those on foot invite us to alight and promenade the Lunetta with them, that we may hear more distinctly the plaintive music of the Indian band.

Our bands at home generally play stirring music for an open-air concert, when crowds are moving about, but here it is soft and sad, the right kind to listen to if you are sitting in a quiet part of the park, looking out to sea, though not easy to appreciate while mingling in the chattering throng, and stopping to shake hands with somebody every few minutes.

On other evenings we go out upon a mole that extends a long way into the bay, and forms a smooth stone walk, where a few people are always sauntering up and down in the twilight. At such times the dreamy enchantment of the Lotus Eaters is upon me; home seems very far off, unreal, and I feel that I would be almost willing to stay forever where " tropic stars look down," and let the "Lyra" return without me. But even if Marion would stay too, could Amy give up her brother Arthur, and all the attractions of her native land for any charm in the Island of Luzon? I think not, Gussie. We drive quickly out to Santa Ana, for romancing on the mole has led us to forget invited dinner company, and among the dark foliage by the roadside the fire-fly trees flash out, sparkling all over like Christmas evergreens lighted up with little candles. I don't know the real name of this peculiar tree that is so attractive to fire-flies, but it forms the prettiest feature of a drive out of town when there is no moonlight.

Last evening we drove to San Gabrielle and San Miguel, two "pueblos," or villages, on the outskirts of the city, and found our homeward way closed up by a torchlight procession in honor of the saints. It was composed of women, chiefly, and large images were borne along on elevated platforms all ablaze with candles.

In a recent drive after dark through a more

distant "pueblo," we were startled by a sudden glare of light that was from no fire-fly tree. Around an Indian hut twenty people were kneeling in silence, each with a lighted candle, for the Last Sacrament was being administered to some dying person within the hut, and these friends were keeping a solemn watch with the departing soul.

At the sunset ringing of the church bells, all good Catholics here pause in whatever they may be doing to repeat a prayer. The men stand with uncovered heads, and some kneel on the wayside grass, while all talking and laughter is hushed for a few minutes. One instance of the peculiar way in which those of the Romish Church can glide from gay pursuits to religious performances and back again, was observable at the Christmas Eve balls. The 25th of December occurred on Sunday, and before the stroke of twelve on Saturday night, all the dancers betook themselves to church for devotional services; then returned to the ball-rooms, and danced until the day was several hours old. Christmas Eve and the Sunday passed quietly with us. There is no Protestant church in this island, and Spanish rule has but lately allowed the existence of a regular burying ground for "heretics." Every Sunday evening there is a little meeting in Mrs. Irvine's parlor, and one in another house nearer town, attended by some who feel it a privilege for even two or three to gather together in Christ's name. There are very few who show interest in them, — only six young men come here for the service; but it is always the pleasantest evening in the week, we think, and after prayers and the reading of a sermon, we all spend an hour by the piano, singing the dear old hymns.

I must not forget to give you an account of a funny adventure that befell us last week. One afternoon Arthur and Mr. Duncan came out in a barouche for us to drive with them, and we took a romantic road that wound among rice fields to the Indian village of San Pedro, and through a narrow pass where the rocks were heavily draped with vines, and feathery bamboos growing on them far above us, bent over in an arch, making a soft green gloom from which we emerged upon the Pasig river. There the road ended, and then it was proposed that we should leave the carriage to return through San Pedro, while we went down the river in a banca, or Indian canoe. Several of them were floating near the bank, and although Marion and I were unsuitably dressed for such an adventure, we could not refuse anything so jolly. Gathering up our white muslins, we crept into the long, narrow canoe with some difficulty, because of its very low roof, and were soon speeding down the river, *apparently*, in high glee at our situation. It might have been more comfortable, for the roof interfered with our view, and Mr. Duncan was obliged to sit in the stern where he could raise his lofty head, and let part of his inconvenient length hang over the side of the banca. With broad paddles our boatmen made swift progress, and when we reached a place where the river branched, our mirth was turned to anxiety, for we asked one of the men which way would bring us to Manila, and he pointed to that by which we had come. This puzzled us, for it was difficult to see how we could have been so mistaken, and at first we did not believe him, but we had lost all idea of locality, and at last allowed him to turn back, and go in the direction that he declared was that of the city. By this time night had come upon us suddenly, as it does in the tropics, and we began to fear we should be carried beyond our landing place. A few lights twinkled from huts among the bamboos on the banks, and every other minute a flash of lightning illumined the dark river.

"We must have been on the way to Lake Bay when we first set out," said Arthur, "and I never had my head so completely turned before. Look out, shipmates, for Santa Ana church, because it is high time to see it, and I shall believe these Indians are taking us to the lake, after all, if we don't discover some familiar landmark soon." "There it is now," said Mr Duncan, his keen eyes first discovering the great building looming up in the dusk. Feeling much relieved, though rather guilty, we soon encountered Mr. and Mrs. Irvine, who had been very much concerned for our safety, as the driver of our barouche had returned a long time before, leaving some indefinite message about the Señores, the Señoritas, and the river.

"Not dinner time yet!" I exclaimed in surprise, seeing the table in the "cayeda" had no adornments of damask and silver. "I thought we were very late." "And so you are," cried our hostess with a dismayed face. "My dear girls, have you forgotten our engagement to dine at the Señora Barreda's to night?" Indeed we had, and with one glance at Mrs. Irvine's elegant costume, and at our draggled muslins, we rushed to our room, and arrayed ourselves for a dinner party in a flurry from which we did not recover until half way into town, when Marion found that she had left her gloves behind during our excited preparations.

We were guests of a Spanish lady that evening, and after saying "buenos noches" to her at first, I was at a loss for any more pure Castilian with which to address her until our departure, when I distinguished myself by bringing out "He tenido una noche muy agradable" (I have had a very pleasant evening). After all the studying during the voyage to San Francisco, should you not have thought I might have had the language at my tongue's end? But six months in China caused my learning to melt away like morning mist; I was either too hot or too much entertained by other things to attend to my "Ollendorf."

There were people enough at the Señora's to talk English with, and the one whom we were invited especially to meet was a pleasant little bride, who came out recently to the Philippines on her father's vessel, and was persuaded by a Scotch merchant to remain here. We always have a good time at these dinner-parties, notwithstanding the disturbing consciousness that if a single lady converses more affably with her right hand neighbor than with the gentleman at the other side, it will be commented upon in various offices next morning, and the fact will be food for much speculation. Those who believe that gossip is altogether within the province of womankind should see how eásily the stronger sex indulge in it, when their minds are not too much encumbered with weightier things.

The best part of the evening to me is the homeward drive near midnight, when such moonlight as we never saw elsewhere illumines our way, for a half moon seems to give as bright a light here as the full orb does in the temperate zone. Banana leaves, half screening the thatched Indian houses, reflect its gleam from their polished surfaces; the warm air is filled with the sweet, heavy perfume of the *Dama des Noches* (Our Lady of the Night), and the three ladies in Mr. Irvine's barouche find little need for any head-covering, or even for thin shawls over their white dresses on these nights in midwinter.

The way that we were taken home after one dinner-party deserves to be described. We went to a house that stands so close to the river that a flower could be tossed into it from its back windows, and found, after leaving the table at half-past nine o'clock, that our host had a little steam-launch in waiting to convey all the company who lived near the Pasig to their homes. This, at least, was his original intention, but it expanded into nothing less than a journey to Lake Bay, twenty miles above the city; and crowded together in the bow of the boat for the purpose of seeing at best advantage the moonlit scenery before us, we steamed on toward the lake, of which we had heard strange tales enough to make it seem like a fabulous place to Marion and myself.

After many windings of the Pasig, our launch came to the entrance of a broad sheet of water, fifteen miles across, and about a hundred in circumference. In the distance were mountains, dimly seen, for the moonlight had become hazy, and after a brief pause we began our return trip at the witching hour of night. The chilly dampness of the air brought shawls into requisition, and jokes did not fly about with such startling velocity as during our upward way, for some of the gentlemen were cold and sleepy, but a good deal of fun was kept up among a few of us until half-past two, when we arrived at Mr. Irvine's house. There the shallow water would not allow a near approach to the shore, and on went the boat to the domain of a neighbor, where they barely succeeded in making a safe landing for ladies by means of a narrow plank, down which we tottered into outstretched arms and found ourselves on dry ground, almost too stiff and tired for a walk of five minutes to our abode.

"After so many gay evenings, one of you girls might have the charity to come off to the ship to-night and console two forlorn fellows," was our captain's plea when he came ashore to see us the next afternoon, and as I had visited the "Lyra" for that benevolent purpose quite recently, Marion said she would accompany him. Our kind host evidently thought she was making a sacrifice to exchange an evening on shore, with the social pleasures of his beautiful and brilliantly lighted "sala," for the melancholy harbor and a ship's cabin, and he followed her to the carriage with persuasive words. "I am *sure* you would stay if you knew who are intending to call to-night, Miss Marion," was the last arrow in his quiver, but her firmness elicited from him the quotation:

> "When a woman will, she will,
> And you may depend on't;
> But when she won't, she won't;
> And there's an end on't,"

which he delivered in a despairing tone as the barouche rolled out through the gateway.

On the quiet upper deck of the "Lyra,"

watching the sunset fade from sky and water, and trying to cheer both captain and mate, who in truth were forlorn, as the former had said, being heartily tired of Manila Bay, Marion called their attention to a steamer that was approaching them. As it anchored quite near, they recognized the English man-of-war "Hanover," from Hong Kong, among whose staff of officers is Lieut. Olney, the gentleman who discussed the Assembly's Catechism with Marion at the musical party in November, and did not appear to have had too much of it on that occasion, as Arthur surmised from the friendliness with which he pursued our acquaintance afterward. Darkness soon hid the steamer from the sight of the trio on the clipper-ship, but through it came a boat to the gangway of the latter, and by light of the deck lantern was revealed the jovial visage of the lieutenant. He was a walking news-bag on this occasion, and regaled them all with the substance of what had been said, done, and contemplated by the hundred (more or less) of our acquaintances in that mountain-walled city since we left it. Then he had to be told what entertainments Manila was able to afford, and declared it would be "a jolly lark" for Captain Roslyn to give a party on the "Lyra," and treat our city friends to a ship supper; the novelty of which, at least, would be sure to please them. Acting on the suggestion we did have an impromptu party the next night, and the fun of it was no less than if it had been longer in contemplation; but there was not quite such a merry-making as upon a similar occasion in California, for the etiquette of Manila would hárdly allow ladies to mount the spanker-boom.

Not believing in the proverb that advises one to do in Rome as the Romans do, we did not attend a bull-fight given here last Sunday, and I do not suppose we missed any great enjoyment, or that you will regret that I cannot give you a description of such an entertainment.

I could spin out this letter indefinitely were I

to describe our visits to shops where the exquisite piña embroidery is sold, or to the old Spanish churches, where are seen the glittering altars and amazing pictures of the saints; or to the houses of Mestizos, to watch torchlight processions from their balconies, or merely to return civilities by a short call; and at such times our conversation with the ladies of the mansion has to be held by means of an interpreter, who knows both Spanish and English. It is not fluent, but generally very funny. I might do better to follow the example of a young American gentleman who made calls with his pocket-dictionary, and would refer to it whenever he was obliged to pause for a word. Above all, I could lengthen this epistle (if it were not too long already) with sketches of many friends who are so agreeable that even Marion's confidence in mankind seems to be reviving. You can hear about them all when we come home, for it will take more stamps than I can well afford to secure the safe transportation of these pages, and I will not add to their number, therefore

    Farewell, from

          AMY.

CHAPTER XIII.

EXCURSION TO PAGSANJAN.

MARION'S STORY.

"*At Sea,*" *Jan.* 21*st,* 18—.

THE "Lyra's" bow is at last turned homeward, and I, on deck this bright afternoon with my writing, have allowed the pen to rest idly in my hand for a long, long time, while watching the dim outlines of Luzon, now fading from our view. Not without regret have I sat here gazing back at that fair island, yet my reverie has been rainbow-tinted, for the memory of happy times is a treasure that cannot be wholly lost; it is something laid up to be glad of and better for in future years.

We stop at Anjer in about ten days to get a pile of letters, as we fondly hope, and this one will be conveyed to you thence by steam, while the winds bear us onward more slowly. At least a hundred days of sea life stretch out between us and the arrival in America, and the sudden cessation of Manila gaieties, with this quiet prospect ahead, gives me the feeling of having suddenly awakened from a remarkable dream.

Of all episodes in our Manila life, the crowning one occurred a week ago, and to ensure my peace of mind for the homeward voyage an account of it must be left at Anjer to speed on to you, or I shall rehearse it to you in imagination both night and day.

I have often watched longingly the little steamer "Dwende" from our corridor, as she came puffing up the river on her trips to Lake Bay, the great lake of which we had only a tantalizing peep when we took that excursion to it after an evening dinner-party, and as we heard descriptions of the great mountain Majajay (pronounced Mahahai) on the farther side, and of the tropic loveliness at its foot, it seemed hard to leave Luzon without going there. There appeared to be no prospect of such a trip, and the time of our departure was drawing near, when an unexpected proposal came from two of our friends, Messrs. Searle and Carleton. If it would be agreeable to Mrs. Irvine and her guests, they had thought of hiring the "Dwende" for an excursion across Lake Bay. In addition to the household at Santa Ana, and the gentlemen from whom the proposal came, the party would comprise Captain Roslyn, and Messrs. Wellington, Flanders, Emerson, Sydney, and Von Prockoroff.

This was indeed a climax to the pleasures of seven weeks! The answer returned was to assure those obliging young men that their design met with our cordial assent, and the next evening as the sun was throwing long, golden rays over the Pasig and its banana groves, there were two expectant maidens out on the "azatere" that overlooks the river, gazing toward the city for the first glimpse of the little "Witch," as in English we designate the steamer "Dwende." A faint strain of music is our first warning of her approach, and as she turns the last curve and stops before the house, we wonder what is that lively air, unknown, yet strangely familiar, which the Indian band on board play with increasing enthusiasm. "What *is* that pretty tune?" I inquire of Mr. Searle, who is conducting me to the river bank, and he asks with some chagrin if I do not recognize my country's melody, "Yankee Doodle," which he, as a special compliment to the ladies from America, had taught to the band leader by singing it to him until he was hoarse. A convulsion seizes me at this, and I nearly fall into the water. Is it the Englishman's imperfect knowledge of our time-honored tune, or the Indian's incorrectness of ear that has caused this air to improve so greatly upon "Yankee Doodle," and

Page 356.

to be hardly more than fourth cousin to it?

But if my friend's musical ability was at fault, I could do justice to his powers as a commissary, when, as the steamer went her way in the gathering darkness, we all repaired to a brightly lighted and bountifully spread dinner-table on the lower deck. The "Dwende" makes no pretensions to convenience or comfort in respect to cabins. She has one small room, which we ladies viewed with disfavor as a place to sleep in, and leaving our travelling-bags there, went to the upper deck after dinner, resolved to spend the night in our chairs rather than be stifled in such a den.

Warmly wrapped in all the shawls and overcoats that could be mustered, our party of twelve steamed across Lake Bay, while Mr. Von Prockoroff's violin music and Mr. Flanders' Scotch songs filled the pauses in our merry talk, and kept drowsiness at a distance until one o'clock in the morning. Then an elderly and lop-sided moon arose over the dark edge of the island Talim, near the middle of the lake, and somebody ventured to suggest that the few hours before sunrise might be profitably spent in sleep.

Two sofas were brought on deck, and arranged in such a way as to form a convenient little nest for Amy and me. Mrs. Irvine dozed in a great chair near us; Arthur rolled up in a rug reposed on the deck, and the others made themselves comfortable in various ways. It seemed as if no more than half an hour could have passed when I started up, and with half-opened eyes saw a great mountain. There was one white cloud floating below its level crest, and the sky was tinted with the soft, pink hue of dawn. The "Dwende" had come to anchor before Majajay, with the village of Santa Cruz at its base, and after an early breakfast we set out in a large banca in quest of adventures. Followed by our Indian band, playing merrily in another canoe, we turned into the Pagsanjan river, far too lovely a stream for such a name (but be sure you pronounce the j as if it were h), and

Excursion to Pagsanjan.

followed its winding course for hours. Its low banks were in some places covered with a thick growth of trees that bent over the water with their weight of luxuriant vines; then we passed wide, level groves of the palm or mango, where opening vistas, bright with sunshine streaming through the branches, darkened, as they converged, into a sombre green, and there were glimpses of distant mountain-tops above all.

Our banca was of sufficient size to accommodate several chairs, which were occupied by the lady excursionists, while the gentlemen sat at their feet and made themselves so agreeable that we might have wished to sail on (paddle I mean) forever, if it had not been for feeling rather stiff and cramped after many miles of river-travelling. As it was, we were quite ready to land, when they proposed it, on a wooded knoll, by which the river makes a sudden turn, and dashes on in a series of wild little rapids between high, rocky walls. Indian boatmen were there with two small bancas, and it was the plan of our leaders to leave our large canoe for these, and mount the rapids. The two frail crafts could not carry all of the party with safety, but all did not care to go, and Amy and myself embarked in one with Mr. Carleton and Mr. Emerson, while four others followed us in an equally small and more ricketty banca.

On both sides of the narrow river steep cliffs towered to the height of three hundred feet. Ferns and moss clothing their rugged sides were kept fresh and brilliantly green by the mist of tiny cascades that leaped out from among them, and, with trailing vines and waving boughs, were reflected in the clear, quiet pools between each rapid, as if in a Claude Lorraine glass. After every one of these still places came a furious little torrent, where the water was shallow enough for the gentlemen to get out and push the banca. Mr. Carleton, armed with a paddle, made violent exertions to battle against the opposing force of the stream, and Mr. Emerson acted as pusher. We girls grasped the sides of our craft to avoid being spilt out, and shrieked with fear and glee combined, thinking that in all our lives we had never been on such a "lark" before.

The water dashed in, and we were getting a soaking, when, coming to a rapid that was more violent than the preceding ones, Mr. Carleton thought we had better get out and walk past it on the rocks — a matter of some difficulty, for they were wet and slippery; but assisted, one at a time, by our guides, we made the pilgrimage, and then rested on a great boulder to watch Mr. Emerson trying to drag the canoe through the rushing water, which almost swept him downward in its course. While we were waiting, the other party joined us, and by the time our banca had been taken through the rapid, and tipped over on one side to let the water pour out, Mr. Searle had concluded to take passage in it; for the other one, he said, was unsafe if heavily laden. Mr. Searle is no trifling weight, and when we went on he bore down the end of the banca where I sat to such an extent that the water came over me in bucketfuls, I might say, and the little craft, turning broadside to the stream, narrowly escaped being swamped.

Another landing on the rocks had to be made, and I proceeded to wring my dress, which had absorbed so much of the Pagsanjan river that its weight nearly dragged me over on my face. There stood poor Marion, looking like a drowned rat; French kid boots, the delight of her heart, entirely ruined; white dress stained a dark brown color about half-way up the skirt, and rivulets pouring from every ruffle. The gentlemen asked us if we would try another rapid, and I would have gone on with joy, for, being already drenched, what did I care for a little extra dampness? But there was a chance for Amy to be a good deal wetter than she was, and deciding to run no more risk, we shot down the river easily to the grove, where waited those of our party who had not ascended the rapids.

"Well! you are sights for an exhibition," were the words that greeted our return; and obviously the next thing to be done was to get dry. Mr. Carleton advised sitting in the sun, and Mr. Searle was positive that to walk up and down would accomplish our end more quickly. Now it is a curious fact that Mr. Searle generally makes me do just what he wants me to, though it may not be with a good grace, and this time we both promenaded the river banks, while, as a poem called the "Excursion" (but not written by Wordsworth) sweetly expresses it:

"From sunstroke they were only saved by an umbrella's shade ;
All stained with mud, a truly dismal spectacle they made."
— *M. Gilmer, Poetess.*

Soon the other boat-load arrived, even more drenched and muddy than we were, and a desire was felt by every body for the provisions that had been sent on before us to the village of Pagsanjan. Therefore were all the excursionists, whether wet, damp, or dry, impelled by hunger to crowd into their large banca, and follow the "parvo y jamon" (turkey and ham) to the place where those edibles were waiting to be consumed.

The house of the principal Indian in the village was hospitably open for our accommodation, and there the dinner-baskets were unpacked, and around the festive board our famished company disposed themselves; not too hungry and tired however, for much merriment during the progress of the meal. At its close graceful speeches were made relative to the ladies from the United States, whose visit to Luzon had occasioned this excursion; and in their behalf Capt. Roslyn rose to make a polite reply.

He gave our companions to understand that if the coming of said ladies to Luzon had given pleasure to any of them, it was in no wise beyond what they themselves experienced in making such delightful acquaintances. It takes Arthur to do up this sort of thing in style, and my opinion is he over-did it. I felt like sticking a pin into him, but unhappily the table was between us; for even if there was a fair amount of

Kulu Girl. — Page 366.

truth in his remarks, did I want those people to believe we thought so much of them that we should sail from Manila the next week with aching hearts?

After dinner came a stroll through the village, and into the venerable Catholic church (such a damaged set I don't think had ever honored Pagsanjan before); then carriages were ready to take us to Santa Cruz, the town near which the "Dwende" lay at anchor. The wide, smooth road led through groves of tall cocoa palms and open paddy fields, and beyond them Majajay rose grandly in the twilight. That was a sober drive for me, because Mr. Searle was my *vis-à-vis* in the barouche, and we did not feel quite serene, or even cheerful. Good friends as we are, it seems to be a peculiarity of ours to aggravate each other every now and then, and during this day we had succeeded in doing it better (or worse) than ever before.

My fault chiefly I knew it was, and felt remorseful, for we owed this charming trip to the thoughtful kindness of Mr. Searle and his friend Carleton, and I had spoilt his enjoyment of it by my contrariness!

The pleasures of the day had been fatiguing, and when once more on board the steamer their effects began to appear in several of our number. First, Mr. Flanders grew pallid, and had to leave the dinner-table on account of faintness, but it would take something more than a slight indisposition to keep his tongue quiet, and on deck during the evening it made itself heard, perhaps a *little* more faintly than usual. Mr. Sydney's share of the Pagsanjan rapids had given him a violent chill, so that he shook from head to foot, and naturally could not be entertaining. Mr. Searle, enveloped in a huge blanket, with even his head buried in its folds, allowed it to emerge once while he favored us with a Spanish song, "Cual mariposa di rosa en rosa," after which his energies collapsed, and he retired from the scene. But my Amy's brilliancy, and that of a few others who vied with her in repartee, had not been quenched by water or clouded by fatigue, and I sat on a cushion, resting my weary head in her lap, and listened to conversation that resembled an exhibition of fire-works, and sometimes I had to start up and send off a feeble rocket on my own account when it became too inspiring for me to keep still.

The next sunrise found us again in the familiar Pasig River, and at Santa Ana the "Dwende's" pleasant party broke up. It re-assembled in a few days to sit for a photograph, because every body wanted to perpetuate the excursion in some form, and we arranged ourselves on a green lawn, with banana leaves for a back-ground, while a Spanish artist fussed over us with his camera for the best part of one afternoon before he could produce a pictured group that satisfied the originals.

Then came our sailing day; it was yesterday, yet Luzon is hardly out of sight now, our progress has been so slow. We were escorted from the Manila quay to a ship by a party of faithful friends who wished to see the last of us, they said, and then contradicted themselves by declaring that they were sorry to do so. A steam launch conveyed us across the harbor to the vessel, where we all tried to be gay after our usual fashion until good-byes had to be said, and some of them were hard to say. It was proposed that all the Pagsanjan party, English, Irish, Scotch, American, and Russian, should meet in 1880 at Niagara Falls to renew their acquaintance, but that hope failed to cheer any body sufficiently, and as one after another descended the gangway, and looked up at us for a second farewell, we thought "it may be for years," but it is far more likely to "be forever."

I trust that I am not growing sentimental, and for fear you may thus accuse me, I will close now with the words that, looking up from my paper, I say to Luzon, sinking below the horizon, and to all those who remember us there, and have watched the "Lyra's" white sails go out to sea, "Adios! adios!"

MARION.

CHAPTER XIV.

HOMEWARD BOUND.

THE little settlement of Anjer nestles among the wide-spreading banyan trees on the southern side of Java. Its red roofed Dutch houses peep out from the dark foliage with suggestions of comfort to be enjoyed on their generous verandahs, where the blinds, shutting out the blazing sun, are drawn up at the day's close to admit the refreshing sea breeze. Mountains, green with never ending summer, form a background to the pretty picture of the town as seen from the water, and the eye follows the curving white shore to the point of the island where a tall light-house stands to ensure the safe passage of vessels through the Straits of Sunda.

On the afternoon of February 1st, 18—, the good ship "Lyra" floated before Anjer, awaiting the return of her captain and passengers, who had gone ashore for their letters, and then, having driven to the lighthouse, were surveying sea and land from an altitude of three hundred feet. Looking downward from that dizzy height upon a garden of brilliant flowers directly below them; and, beyond, on the land-ward side, over a verdant country, sloping upwards into mountains of velvet green, Amy and Marion stood entranced, taking a mental retrospect of nine months in the beautiful East, while below waited their noble vessel to bear them over the wide ocean to their far-off home.

Amy, leaning on the iron railing, her brown eyes shining with deep happiness, sang softly the closing words of a grand oratorio, "We praise Thee now and evermore."

Anjer. — Page 375.

With precious packages of letters the three voyagers left the shores of Java, as moonbeams were glistening on the waves over which their boat sped to the waiting ship, that, with her sails set, drifted slowly from them, as if impatient to begin the long homeward passage; and as they climbed her gangway the girls said to each other, "When we go down these steps again it will be with a last leave-taking to the 'Lyra.'"

For a hundred days, at least, their home was to be upon the deep, and that those days should be profitably spent was the determination of Capt. Roslyn's companions, and not only with regard to themselves. They meant that the voyage should be time improved to that young man as well. They knew he had the best of reasons for longing to reach American shores, where was a magnet toward which his heart turned as truly as the needle of his compass to the North, and those young females, with wisdom beyond their years, determined upon a course of treatment for his case. With two ends in view — to keep him from thinking unduly about America, and themselves from indulging harmfully in Manila reminiscences, they set to work to improve their minds, and his, too. The captain had injured his eyes by taking lunar observations, and the days would have been very long to him had it not been for his indefatigable sister and cousin, who made him learn with the help of their eyes whatever they learned, and listen to whatever they wanted to read. Perhaps he might have chosen more romances than they considered profitable, but they always kept some light literature on hand to be taken like maple sugar after Peruvian bark, never treating him to it, however, until a good dose of deep reading and study had been faithfully administered.

Captain Arthur could listen with equanimity to the "Life of Rufus Choate," and the "Memoirs of Henry Crabb Robinson." His special dread was a book of general information that

Marion insisted on his committing to memory with her as a mental tonic.

"You can't feel romantic when I am cramming this book into both our heads at once," said Marion, in answer to his protestations, "and no more can I, so don't you say a word against it."

In spite of these afflicting circumstances Captain Roslyn was not greatly to be pitied, for his girls had some compassion in their hearts, and amused him with zeal as great as that with which they gave him tonics. Exciting games of chess on deck shortened the afternoons so much that four bells (six o'clock) struck by the man at the wheel, and the prompt ringing of the tea-bell in the cabin often came as a surprise to the players.

Lovely evenings those were in the Indian Ocean, famed for its sunsets, where the monarch of the day calls for admiring and oft-times awed attention as he sinks below the far blue water-line. One evening they must watch the snow-white cloud masses in the East glowing with reflected crimson and then turning to gray; at an other time they wonder at the deep, translucent blue, dotted with ashes of roses, while westward stretches a flaming sheet of red and gold, and when the sky has faded and moonlight whitens the sails, Amy brings her guitar, and with its vibrating cords the murmuring waves join in to follow her sweet voice.

Or sometimes, instead of listening to ballads, they join in singing hymns, Mr. Duncan lending his deep bass to make up a quartette, whose music causes the sailors on the lower deck to tread softly and lower their tones. If a sudden shower disperses the singers, they gather around the cabin organ, and perhaps end the evening with a reading-circle under the swinging lamp.

That no one need imagine these favored voyagers to be wholly exempt from annoyance, it should be stated that their happy evenings terminated with a fierce warfare waged against cockroaches in their respective state-rooms. A cargo of sugar ensures the presence of these insects, who only keep quiet in the daytime to be livelier tormentors at night, and a black roach, measuring from one to two inches, who may spread his wings and fly at your head if the notion seizes him, is not the best company to induce sleep.

Amy and Marion, in opposite rooms, are armed with slippers, which descend with resounding whacks upon the prey, and a shriek frequently testifies to the escape of some swift insect, while the captain dances about his little office, flapping a wet towel at one or two flying specimens. One night when they had all retired, Amy's door opened hastily, and she called "Marion, do come here — quick! I've got a great worm with horns in my room." The intruder proved to be a centipede, but he was apparently without kith or kin on board the ship; certainly none of his kind was seen again in the cabin.

It will not do to omit mentioning the new passenger who sailed from Manila in the "Lyra," for she was considered a member of the family-party quite as much as Mr. Duncan. A small Spanish poodle, deaf, and rather stupid, yet very pretty, with her pathetic brown eyes and curly white hair, had been the parting gift of a friend, and Marion, who always denounced the folly of a woman's petting small dogs, could not resist the loving ways of this one, any more than the rest did who opened their hearts wide to little "Luna." When she was discovered one day with a family of four some dismay was expressed, and the question, "What can we do with so many dogs?" was asked, but never answered in words. They were suffered to live, however, and when all were on their legs it was difficult to cross the cabin without stepping on a soft, woolly ball that squealed piteously at the attention. The girls read, studied, and worked with Toddles and Poddles (named after the twins in "Our Mutual Friend"), and Fleecy and Posy actually swarming over them, and Luna generally lying close to one of her friends with her nose on the book, or her paw on the sewing. Amy seemed to attract the quadrupeds more than any one; they loved to gather round her, and nestle in the folds of her dress when she was sitting in a low easy chair, and it was a pretty sight when the row of sleeping poodles upon the hem of a certain blue dress, the captain's favorite, made it appear like a robe bordered with white fur.

Calm days often tried the captain's patience, and he was almost ready to scold his girls for not being in so great a hurry as he was to get home; but the springs of his good nature were too deep for him to be readily irritated, even by the flapping of the sails — that sound so trying to a sailor's nerves and temper — and any amusement that they found to beguile these still times he would join in, whistling perseveringly for a breeze meanwhile. One afternoon, when the sea was like azure satin for smoothness and shining color, a fleet of nautili were noticed sailing along under the shadow of the vessel, and designs quickly made upon them were only given up after long and patient fishing with a bucket and rope. Each tiny voyager in his fragile boat floated by the snare, and as the three heads bending over the rail were raised at last, a sudden breeze ruffled the quiet deep, and bore to them something not quite briny — hardly an odor, but a suggestion of land.

"Now, we smell Africa!" cried Captain Roslyn, "and we are not far from it. Girls, take a long breath, and imagine forests over in the direction this wind comes from. The calm is over, and I'm a happy man again."

It was over, indeed, for that time, and a gale in store for them. In two days the changeable ocean lifted up its waves and took on a wild appearance, the heaving surface streaked all over with white, while great breakers came rolling up behind the stern, pitching the ship forward in the deep hollows, from which her bow rose triumphantly, shaking off the water from its figurehead, the nymph with a lyre in her arms. A strong, cold wind blew the spray like drifting snow in the faces of the girls as they stood by the taffrail, finding it difficult to keep their balance unless clinging with both arms, yet too much in the spirit of the scene to go below to safer and warmer quarters. The captain finally seized a rope, and passing it around their waists, bound them firmly to the railing. Finding them after dark sitting on the steps of the companion-way that led up on deck, and despatching enormous green pickles, he inquired what set their avaricious minds to covet the sailors' especial stores.

"Won't the cabin pickles satisfy you, without stealing from the poor shell-backs?" he demanded.

"Oh, they can't compare with these!" they cried. "Mr. Duncan got them for us, and on such nights as this we must have something sour."

"Are my brave sailor girls sea-sick?" asked Captain Roslyn, suspiciously.

"No, indeed; only 'kind o' funny,' as Nora the stewardess used to say; and who wouldn't be on a ship acting as this one does to-night!"

The captain was forced to confess that even he was near that state of disturbance in which pickles are the first requirement, and he joined their feast on the steps. After this, when a gale came it was made an excuse to eat pickles, and the supply in the sailors' keg would soon have been low if fairer weather had not set in before they saw Cape of Good Hope light.

On a pleasant Sunday morning Table Mountain appeared, and all day was plainly seen. No table could present a more level surface than that wide mountain top, as seen from a distance of several miles. "It would be nice to play croquet there if it were as flat and smooth as it looks," was the girls' comment upon it.

The island of St. Helena was the next point of interest on the homeward voyage. Looming up from the horizon, the bare, rocky side by which the "Lyra" approached it gives the idea of a frowning fortress — a safe prison for the emperor who made Europe tremble. On that side there is one enormous square rock called " The Barn," more than a thousand feet high ; and far above it on green heights, is Longwood, where the captive Napoleon looked out from among the trees upon the track of passing vessels. Rounding the corner of the " Barn," they saw Jamestown at the foot of towering hills, and a few vessels at anchor before it. Captain Roslyn set out in his boat to visit one of them, the English man-of-war " Rattlesnake," and returned after some hazard, caused by a rough sea and leaky boat, with London papers and a few cabbages and potatoes ; and then they sailed away from the historic island, leaving it bathed in a flood of afternoon sunlight.

St. Helena passed, there was nothing for our voyagers to anticipate but the Highlands of Neversink, and they went on as before to improve the time, and enjoy each other's society. Services were held in the cabin every Sunday, and on Wednesday evenings the sailors' Bible class. Passengers were not admitted to the latter, but a deep interest in it, rather than idle curiosity, sometimes led them to look down through the skylight upon the cabin table, gathered around which the men pored over their Testaments, some whose knitted brows testified to the difficulty of their task in making out a few verses; others, with earnest upturned faces, listened to their captain as he made the truths of God clear to them. Saturday evenings were frequently devoted to simple lectures upon such subjects as mariners must find it desirable to understand, though comparatively few have any but vague ideas of them—trade winds, for example, on one Saturday; cyclones, the Gulf Stream, and astronomy on succeeding weeks, and all set forth so clearly that the youngest lad could not fail to understand what was said, while an occasional pleasantry of the captain's never failed to excite a broad grin upon the weather-beaten faces. Before the end of the voyage the series was closed by a temperance lecture, designed as a preparation for the temptations soon to assail them in port.

At last came a day, the one hundred and seventeenth of their passage, when the Highlands outside of New York harbor rose from the sea — a signal to the inmates of the "Lyra" that the end of their happy voyage drew near. Staten Island, covered with the fresh verdure of May, was a welcome sight to eyes long used only to the blue of water and sky; never had grass looked so green to them as that around the forts, and on all sides the land seemed rejoicing in Spring-time. What a change from ocean solitude was the busy life and stir of that wide harbor! The white pilot-boats, skimming by like fleet-winged birds, outward bound steamers crowded with passengers for Europe, puffing ferries, threading their way among the anchored or moving vessels, and beyond all, the great metropolis to which, nineteen months before, the girls had bidden farewell.

New York's tall spires were rosy with sunset as the "Lyra" moved slowly up to the dock. There Amy and Marion saw dear familiar faces watching the ship's approach with as much longing and eagerness as if she brought them the treasures of the East, and soon her cabins resounded with welcoming voices.

So the girls' voyage ended, and they returned to home scenes and duties with a new song of gladness and praise in their hearts — a stronger desire to be useful and faithful in all future paths of life.

Many a time they may realize that it is easier to go round the world than to go through it; but believing the Divine Presence who led them so safely will not fail them, even unto the end of life's journey, they need fear nothing. May that be true of them which was written of some disciples long ago, who, having known that Presence with them on the deep — "when they had brought their ships to land, followed Him."

THE END.

ENTERPRISE.

We copy the following from *The American Bookseller*, New York:

Few people can have failed to notice the great enterprise, if they have not observed the scrupulous care with which Messrs. D. Lothrop & Co. have published a class of books adapted to the highest culture of the people.

It is only ten years since they commenced the work of publishing, and their list now numbers more than six hundred volumes.

We are glad to make record, that brave and persistent following of a high ideal has been successful.

Messrs. D. Lothrop & Co. have given special attention to the publication of books for children and youths, rightly considering that in no department is *the best*, as regards literary excellence and purity of moral and religious reading, of so great importance. Yet the names of works by such authors as Austin Phelps, D.D., Francis Wayland, and Dr. Nehemiah Adams on their catalogue, will show that maturer readers have not been uncared for.

Of their work projected for the coming season, we have not room to speak in detail; it will suffice for the present to say that it is wide in range, including substantial and elegantly illustrated books, all in the line of the practical and useful, and fresh in character and treatment.

Their two juvenile magazines, *Wide Awake* and *Babyland*, are warmly welcomed in every part of the English-speaking world.

We advise any of our readers who desire to know more about these publications, to send to D. Lothrop & Co., Boston, for an illustrated catalogue.

All who visit their establishment, corner of Franklin and Hawley streets, will not only be courteously welcomed and entertained, but will have the pleasure of seeing one of the most spacious and attractive bookstores in the country.

SUGAR PLUMS. Poems by ELLA FARMAN. Pictures by Miss C. A. Northam. Price, $1 00. D. Lothrop & Co., Boston.

This collection of sweets, which the critics say is the best verse-book published since "Lilliput Levee," will probably prove to be one of the most popular Christmas-Tree books of the season. The poems are written from a child's own point-of-view, and some of them, like "Learning to Count," "Baby's Frights," "Pinkie-Winkie-Posie-Bell," will be perennial favorites in the nursery. While the book is sure to captivate the baby-memory, we will whisper to the mothers that there is not an idle "jingle" in the volume, but that every verse will subtly give a refining and shaping touch to the little child-soul. The book is attractively bound, handsomely illustrated, and ought to be found in every Christmas Stocking in the land.

Ask your Bookseller for it.

POEMS IN COMPANY WITH CHILDREN.—By MRS. S. M. B. PIATT. Illustrated. Price, $1 50. D. Lothrop & Co., Boston.

A mother's book—one of those dainty, treasured volumes of poetry which naturally find a resting-place in the mother's work-basket, always at hand, to be taken up in a tender moment. It also contains many poems to be read aloud in the twilight hour when the children gather around mother's knee. Of its literary excellence it is needless to speak as Mrs. Piatt stands at the head of American women poets.

LINKS IN REBECCA'S LIFE. By "Pansy." Price, $1.50. Boston: D. Lothrop & Co.

"Pansy" has no rival as an author of the best class of Sunday-school books. Her "Ester Ried" and "Chautauqua Girls" series are models in that important line of literature. Her new book, "Links in Rebecca's Life," is worthy of a place in the same list. This book is an admirable one. Its tone is healthy and stimulating, without a trace of sentimentalism or cant: and its characters are thoroughly natural, such as any reader can recognize in the community in which be happens to live. The heroine, Rebecca, is intensely human, with a noble nature in which many weaknesses hide themselves and come often to the surface. But she is a Christian of the best type, and her aspirations and hard-fought battles inspire enthusiasm in a reader. The Committee on International Lessons couldn't do a better thing than to circulate this book in every part of the land. It shows how the lessons may be made helpful in the daily life, and how the Old Testament may be taught with interest to an Infant School, or to men and women of every congregation.

ECHOING AND RE-ECHOING. By *Faye Huntington*. Price $1.50. Boston: D. Lothrop & Co., publishers.

It shows great ignorance of the Sunday-school literature of our day, when one calls it weak and namby-stuff, with an equal mixture of love-stories, and impossible adventures. The censure is just for a certain class of books, but a large library may be gathered of first-class works admirable alike in moral tone and in literary execution, books which everybody can read with delight and profit. "Echoing and Re-echoing" is a book of this sort, a well-told story, abounding with practical lessons, and inciting to a noble Christian life. The most intelligent opponent of religious novels will find his prejudices giving way in reading it, and a fastidious literary reader will be thankful that children have such good books for moulding their literary tastes.

THE CHAUTAUQUA GIRLS AT HOME.—
By *Pansy*. Author of "Four Girls at Chautauqua,," &c.
Boston: D. LOTHROP & Co. Price, $1.50.

The four brilliant young ladies, three from the highest social ranks, and one a teacher with infidel tendencies, who, having abandoned Newport and Saratoga for Chautauqua Lake and its Sunday-school Assembly, were there converted, and, having returned to their city homes, with their simple faith and joyous experience, they enter the First Church, seeking Christian help and a field for usefulness. Hesitatingly they enter the Sunday-school. Their presence there is almost resented by pastor and superintendent, who knew of their former lives of social vaporing, but did not know of their conversion. The rebuff does not wholly dishearten the young ladies. They go to the social meetings, where their persistent attendance brings about an explanation. They confess Christ, are received into the Church, enter into its work with zeal, and by their efforts and influence remodel the Sunday-school, stir up the social meetings, and help to bring about a great revival.

These young ladies in their developing lives represent four classes of Christians, with which every pastor has to deal, and from studying these models pastors can learn helpful lessons, for they are here depicted with a masterly skill. The *First Church* is a representative *dead* Church. The decayed members and the cause of death are pointed out. The question of social amusements for Christians is discussed and answered from the Bible. The Sunday-school is dull and inefficiently managed. How to improve it and make it a success is indicated in a practical way. In short, the whole case of spiritually dead Churches is diagnosticated with the wisdom of a practical physician, and the revivifying remedies prescribed. Pastors, superintendents, teachers, Christians, young and old, should read this book. It contains help for all. "Pansy" has written nothing better — *N. Y. Christian Advocate.*

THE NAME ABOVE EVERY NAME. In sending forth a new and revised edition of this work the Publishers append a few of the many favorable notices which, from various sources, testify to its catholicity, and its adaptation to the wants of the disciples of our Lord by whatever denominational name they may be called.

The Name above Every Name. *or, Devotional Meditations.* WITH A TEXT FOR EVERY DAY IN THE YEAR. By the *Rev. Samuel Cutler.*

This little volume, which is a gem of typography, is just what it claims to be—"devotional and practical." The pure gold of the gospel is here without the base alloy of man's wisdom. It accords with the teachings of the divine Spirit, and tends to exalt in the souls of men the Christ of God.

The texts are fitly chosen, and the exquisite fragments of sacred poetry seem like jewels from a mine of inspiration. None can read this book devoutly without being benefited; and all who read it in the spirit in which it appears to have been written, will lay down the volume with higher views of Christ's nature, and of His work, and reverently acknowledge that if His name be above every name in dignity and glory, it is also, as declared in the inspired canticle, "as ointment poured forth" in its heavenly fragrance.—*Parish Visitor.*

From the Congregationalist.

The Name above Every Name. It has a chapter for every week in the year, each chapter preceded with appropriate passages from Scripture and closing with a choice selection from devotional poetry. The whole book is eminently evangelical, and fitted to foster the growth of true and genuine piety in the soul.

The Name above Every Name. By the *Rev. Samuel Cutler.* This has been carefully prepared by its author. The texts are for every day in the year, and have reference to the Scriptural titles of our Lord. The devotional and practical meditations are for every week in the year. The appendix contains five hundred and twenty five titles of our Lord, with the Scriptural reference; also a topical and alphabetical list of the titles, and of first lines of poetry with the author's name.

The work is exceedingly valuable, not only for its meditations, but for the great amount of information which it contains. It is a book which the Christian would do well always to have at hand. *Evagelical Knowledge Society.*

The volume is a precious *vade mecum*, for all who love the "Name that is above every name"—*Protestant Churchman.*

Plain Edition $1.00   Full Gilt $1.50   Red line Edition $2.00

D. Lothrop & Co., Publishers, Boston.

BOOKS FOR YOUNG HEROES AND BRAVE WORKERS.

VIRGINIA. By *W. H. G. Kingston.* 16 mo. Illustrated $1 25
A stirring story of adventure upon sea and land.

AFRICAN ADVENTURE AND ADVENTURERS. By *Rev. G. T. Day, D. D.* 16 mo. Illustrated . . . . - . 1 50
The stories of Speke, Grant, Baker, Livingstone and Stanley are put into simple shape for the entertainment of young readers.

NOBLE WORKERS. Edited by *S. F. Smith, D. D.* 16mo. 1 50

STORIES OF SUCCESS. Edited by *S. F. Smith, D. D.* 16mo 1 50
Inspiring biographies and records which leave a most wholesome and enduring effect upon the reader.

MYTHS AND HEROES. 16 mo. Illustrated. Edited by *S. F. Smith, D. D.* . 1 50

KNIGHTS AND SEA KINGS. Edited by *S. F. Smith, D. D.* 12mo. Illustrated . 1 50
Two entertaining books, which will fasten forever the historical and geographical lessons of the school-room firmly in the student's mind.

CHAPLIN'S LIFE OF BENJAMIN FRANKLIN. 16mo. Illustrated 1 50

LIFE OF AMOS LAWRENCE. 12mo. Ill. 1 50
Two biographies of perennial value. No worthier books were ever offered as holiday presents for our American young men.

WALTER NEAL'S EXAMPLE. By *Rev. Theron Brown.* 16 mo. Illustrated . . 1 25
Walter Neal's Example is by Rev. Theron Brown, the editor of that very successful paper, *The Youth's Companion.* The story is a touching one, and is in parts so vivid as to seem drawn from the life.—*N. Y. Independent.*

TWO FORTUNE-SEEKERS. Stories by *Rossiter Johnson, Louise Chandler Moulton, E. Stuart Phelps, Ella Farman,* etc. Fully illustrated 1 50

www.ingramcontent.com/pod-product-compliance
Lightning Source LLC
Chambersburg PA
CBHW032009220426
43664CB00006B/186